Always
Prepared

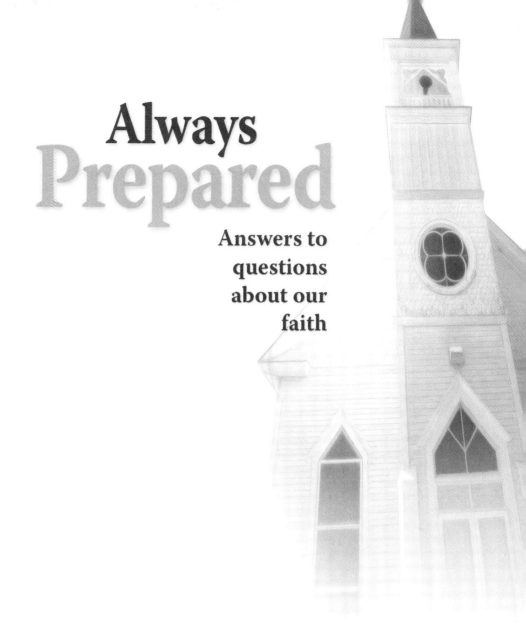

Always Prepared

Answers to questions about our faith

Edited by HUMBERTO M. RASI and NANCY J. VYHMEISTER

Pacific Press® Publishing Association
Nampa, Idaho
Oshawa, Ontario, Canada
www.pacificpress.com

Cover design by Steve Lanto
Cover resources from iStockphoto & www.dreamstime.com
Inside design by Nicola Johnson

Copyright © 2012 by Pacific Press® Publishing Association
Printed in the United States of America
All rights reserved

The authors assume full responsibility for the accuracy of all facts and quotations as cited in this book.

You can obtain additional copies of this book by calling toll-free 1-800-765-6955 or by visiting http://www.adventistbookcenter.com.

Scripture quotations marked ESV are from The Holy Bible, English Standard Version® (ESV®), copyright © 2001 by Crossway, a publishing ministry of Good News Publishers. Used by permission. All rights reserved.
Scripture quotations marked HCSB are taken from the Holman Christian Standard Bible ©, copyright © 1999, 2000, 2002, 2003 by Holman Bible Publishers. Used by permission. Holman Christian Standard Bible ©, Holman CSB ©, and HCSB © are federally registered trademarks of Holman Bible Publishers.
Scripture quoted from NASB are from *The New American Standard Bible*®, copyright © 1960, 1962, 1963, 1968, 1971, 1972, 1973, 1975, 1977, 1995 by The Lockman Foundation. Used by permission.
Scripture quotations marked NIV are from the HOLY BIBLE, NEW INTERNATIONAL VERSION®. Copyright © 1984 by International Bible Society. Used by permission of Zondervan Publishing House. All rights reserved.
Scriptures quoted from NKJV are from The New King James Version, copyright © 1979, 1980, 1982, Thomas Nelson, Inc., Publishers.
Scripture taken from the HOLY BIBLE, TODAY'S NEW INTERNATIONAL VERSION®. Copyright © 2001, 2005 by International Bible Society®. Used by permission of International Bible Society®. All rights reserved worldwide.
Scripture quotations marked KJV are from the King James Version.
Scriptures quoted from RSV are from the Revised Standard Version of the Bible, copyright © 1946, 1952, 1971 by the Division of Christian Education of the National Council of the Churches of Christ in the U.S.A. Used by permission.

Library of Congress Cataloging-in-Publication Data:
Always prepared : answers to questions about our faith / Humberto M. Rasi and Nancy J. Vyhmeister, co-editors.
    p. cm.
ISBN 13: 978-0-8163-2502-3
ISBN 10: 0-8163-2502-2
1. Seventh-day Adventists—Apologetic works—Miscellanea. I. Rasi, H. M. (Humberto M.) II. Vyhmeister, Nancy J.
BX6154.A5636 2012
230'.732—dc23

                                                   2011036813

12 13 14 15 16   •   5 4 3 2 1

Contents

Introduction	7
1 How Reliable Is the Bible? RICHARD M. DAVIDSON	13
2 What Does It Mean to Say That the Bible Is "Inspired"? JO ANN DAVIDSON	27
3 To What Extent Do Archaeological Discoveries Confirm the Bible? RANDALL W. YOUNKER	38
4 Why Do I Believe in God? CLIFFORD GOLDSTEIN	48
5 Are Faith and Reason Compatible? HUMBERTO M. RASI	59
6 What's Unique About Jesus? WILLIAM G. JOHNSSON	69
7 Did Jesus Really Come Back to Life? DAVID MARSHALL	79
8 How Can Miracles Be Possible? KWABENA DONKOR	90

9	Is the God of the Old Testament Different From the One in the New Testament? GREG A. KING	101
10	How Is It That We Do Not Worship Three Gods? JOHN W. REEVE	109
11	What's So Special About the Seventh Day of the Week? WERNER K. VYHMEISTER	121
12	Are There Moral Absolutes? LARRY L. LICHTENWALTER	130
13	If God Is Good and All-powerful, How Can He Allow Suffering? STEPHEN BAUER	141
14	What Happens to Us After We Die? EKKEHARDT MUELLER	152
15	Does God Know the Future? RANKO STEFANOVIC	163
16	Aren't All Religions Basically the Same? BRUCE L. BAUER	173
17	Does It Really Matter What I Believe as Long as I Am Sincere? PAUL DYBDAHL	183
18	How Can I Find Salvation and Eternal Life? WOODROW W. WHIDDEN	192
19	Why Am I a Seventh-day Adventist? NANCY J. VYHMEISTER	201
20	Who Was Ellen White? MERLIN D. BURT	210

Introduction

Most human beings are inquisitive and seek something beyond themselves that will give meaning and purpose to their lives. Through the centuries, men and women have chosen myths, religions, philosophies, or political ideologies to serve as the basis of their convictions, decisions, and their lives on this planet. Thoughtful people have examined the ideas and options available to them to find a core of beliefs they can affirm as trustworthy and embrace as true. Of course, relativists deny the existence of truth, agnostics attempt to remain uncommitted, and postmoderns maintain that even if truth exists, it lies beyond human reach. But a philosophy that denies the possibility of truth undermines its own validity, and reality forces fence-sitters to make ethical choices in real life on a daily basis.

When beginning our search for a reliable set of beliefs with which to guide our lives and on which we can base our moral choices, we must decide between either a natural or a supernatural explanation for the existence of the universe and life. A supernatural explanation leads us either to a myth or a religion. However, a naturalistic explanation—

that matter and life arose spontaneously from nothing and evolved progressively by blind chance and natural laws—is also mythical or quasi-religious, since it requires a belief in the miraculous.

The search for truth

All religions claim to hold and communicate truth, but not all can be equally true. All may be false or only one might be true because their beliefs contradict one another. If all are proven false, we revert to a relativistic or agnostic position. However, if one of them can be true, we must evaluate its truth claims. Do the claims offer satisfactory answers to our deepest questions and yearnings? Are its beliefs internally coherent and applicable to real life situations? Does it provide evidence that appeals to our reason? Do its true followers live worthwhile lives? The answers to these questions are vitally important because the way we live our lives is generally illustrative of what we hold to be true, and furthermore, because the ultimate validity of these truths will determine what happens to us now and at the end of life.

Christianity is a religion that makes specific truth claims. Its Founder, Jesus Christ, appealed to the Scriptures and to His own actions as evidence of the truths He lived and taught (John 5:39, 40). He anticipated that His followers would fight their major battles on the terrain of the human mind. It is in this arena that arguments are weighed and conclusions are reached—where reason and will are engaged. He was also aware of the great potential for ideas to transform us. "You will know the truth," He said, "and the truth will set you free" (John 8:32, NIV). And He added, "I am . . . the truth" (John 14:6, NIV). This leads us inevitably to examine the reliability of the Bible as a trustworthy document and to assess the consistency and lasting impact of Jesus' teachings on His followers and the world at large.

Introduction

Furthermore, the apostle Peter challenged Christians with these words:

"Do not be frightened." But in your hearts set apart Christ as Lord. Always be prepared to give an answer to everyone who asks you to give the reason for the hope that you have. But do this with gentleness and respect, keeping a clear conscience (1 Peter 3:14–16, NIV).

In this short passage, Peter outlined our Christian responsibilities as we prayerfully relate to and interact with our family members, neighbors, friends, and colleagues who may not share our faith convictions.

- *Be prepared.* We must be acquainted with the prevalent ideas of our time and the arguments used against biblical Christianity. Before getting deep into a religious discussion, we should explore some of the general assumptions of the person with whom we are in dialogue.
- *Give reasons.* We must be able to articulate an explanation for our basic beliefs so they can be understood and evaluated by others, and also respond to the common objections against biblical Christianity. Our arguments should be consistent and based on reasonable evidence.
- *Our faith commitment.* The Christian trust and hope centers on the Person of Jesus Christ—His divinity, the truth of His existence and actions, and the reliability of His teachings and promises.
- *Everyone who asks.* Our explanations must be attuned to the one to whom we are speaking, whose ideas may range from those of an

honest seeker to those of an astute critic. That person may lack a formal education or possess a postdoctoral degree.
- *Do it with gentleness.* We should present our convictions with courtesy and respect, and be open to dialogue. Truth may be rejected simply because it is communicated in an arrogant or condescending manner.
- *A clear conscience.* Our reasons and explanations may not persuade the other person during the discussion, but may have a greater and longer-lasting impact if our words and our behavior are consistent.
- *Our focus and goal.* The ultimate purpose of our interaction, beyond communicating specific aspects of our faith, is to lead our interlocutor to know and accept Jesus Christ as Savior and Lord of his or her life.

The purpose of this book

This book articulates twenty common questions that Bible-believing Christians encounter regarding their beliefs as they progress in their studies, pursue advanced degrees, and interact with other professionals. The coeditors, in addition to contributing two of the chapters, have assembled an international group of experienced authors, educators, and researchers who have provided thoughtful answers to these foundational questions. Each author, naturally, assumes responsibility for the content of the chapter that bears her or his name.

All contributors share several convictions: that the biblical record is a reliable document on which our faith is anchored; that the Scriptures reveal a wise and powerful God who cares deeply about each human being; and, that God has given us sufficient evidence to place our trust in Him. In other words, that faith and reason are not incompatible. We agree

Introduction

that biblical Christianity can stand up to scrutiny, and, at the same time, that our comprehension of total truth is limited and progressive. In fact, God is honored when we seek to understand and love Him with all of our minds (Matthew 22:37), and He is always ready to lead us "into all truth" (John 16:13).

We also believe that the Bible conveys the broad contours of a metanarrative that includes seven key moments in universal history: (1) at some point in the remote past, God creates a perfect universe and populates it with intelligent and free creatures; (2) an exalted creature rebels against God's principles and, after a struggle, is banished to earth with his followers; (3) during one week in the recent past, God makes this planet habitable and creates plant and animal life, including the first pair of humans, who are endowed with free will; (4) tempted by the rebel creature, the first couple disobeys God and the entire web of life on this planet suffers the consequences, including a devastating global flood; (5) Jesus Christ, the Creator Himself, comes to earth to rescue fallen humans, offering them free salvation and power to live transformed lives; (6) at the end of time, Christ returns in glory, as promised, and grants eternal life to those who have accepted His free offer of forgiveness and salvation; and (7) after a millennium passes, Christ returns to execute final judgment and restores the entire creation to its original perfection, a state which will last forever.

This book, then, is addressed to Christians interested in the rational arguments that support their personal faith and who wish to communicate them to friends and colleagues in a reasonable manner, while helping to remove obstacles to faith in the minds of nonbelievers. It is also addressed to those who wish to learn more about the basic beliefs held by Christians in general and, in particular, by Seventh-day Adventists. The authors and editors have attempted to provide clear and honest answers based on their own studies, reflections, and life experiences with the purpose of reaching a broad circle of readers.

Our gratitude

We wish to express our deep appreciation to each of the contributors to this volume for willingly sharing their expertise and preparing their contributions while actively involved in responsibilities related to research, teaching, and administration. Of course, more questions might have been posed, but those we have chosen will serve as samples of an approach to faith issues from a coherent and integrated biblical worldview perspective. We thank Jerry D. Thomas, vice president for product development at Pacific Press®, who supported this project from its inception and encouraged us along the way.

We also thank you, dear reader, for devoting time to this book and trust that its chapters will help you to find a deeper understanding of truth, which in turn will lead you to a more hope-filled life.

As we begin to explore together the issues, questions, and answers contained in this book, we leave you with the profound wisdom of this ancient prayer:

From cowardice that shrinks from new truth,
From laziness that is content with half-truths,
From the arrogance that thinks it knows all truth—
O God of truth, deliver us!
            Author Unknown

Humberto M. Rasi and Nancy W. Vyhmeister
Loma Linda and Yucaipa, California

RICHARD M. DAVIDSON

Chapter 1

How Reliable Is the Bible?

Throughout the history of the Christian era, and in particular since the time of the eighteenth-century Enlightenment, many skeptics have called into question the reliability of the Bible. The recent rise of postmodernism has brought about a new round of questioning regarding Scripture's reliability. In this essay we examine various lines of evidence supporting the conclusion that the Bible is indeed reliable.

The Bible's self-testimony and inner validation of its reliability

The Bible claims to be fully trustworthy and reliable, because it insists that its message ultimately comes from God Himself. In the Old Testament, there are about sixteen hundred occurrences of four Hebrew words (in four different phrases with slight variations) that explicitly indicate that God has spoken: (1) "declares [n^e'um,$ literally "the utterance of"] the Lord," (2) "thus says the Lord," (3) "and God spoke," and (4) "the word of the Lord."[1] Various Old Testament writers claim that what is written in Scripture is fully reliable truth (2 Samuel 7:28; Nehemiah 9:13; Psalms 19:9; 119:142, 160; Proverbs 22:21; Daniel 10:21). The primary Hebrew words for "truth," *'emunah* and *'emet,* imply the specific nuance of "reliability."[2] Jesus Himself unhesitatingly affirmed the reliability of Scripture: "Your word is truth" (John 17:17); "Scripture cannot be broken" (John 10:35). New Testament writers insist that Scripture is inspired by God and thus is fully reliable (2 Timothy 3:16; 2 Peter 1:21).

Textual reliability

We first look at the reliability of the manuscripts of the biblical text in its original languages of Hebrew and Aramaic (Old Testament) and Greek (New Testament). The history of the textual transmission of Scripture reveals how carefully and painstakingly the biblical text has been preserved down through the centuries to the present day. With regard to the Old Testament, during the decades of the twentieth century prior to the end of World War II, critical scholars had a very low estimate of the accuracy of the received (Masoretic) Hebrew/Aramaic text, since its earliest manuscript dated back only to about A.D. 900 and critical editions of the Hebrew Bible proposed thousands of conjectured emendations to the text. But since 1947 and the discovery of the Dead Sea Scrolls (DSS), which contained manuscripts or fragments of every Old Testament book except Esther, scholars have been amazed to discover how the Masoretes handed down virtually without change the textual tradition from a thousand years earlier. As Bruce Waltke puts it: "The presence of a text type among the DSS (c. 200 B.C. to A.D. 100) identical with the one preserved by the Masoretes, whose earliest extant MS [manuscript] dates to c. A.D. 900, gives testimony to the unbelievable achievement of some scribes in faithfully preserving the text."[3]

With regard to the New Testament, the amount of manuscript evidence for the Greek text is far more abundant than for any other document of the ancient world. There are more than five thousand Greek manuscripts of part or all of the New Testament text, some two thousand ancient Greek lectionaries (NT readings arranged in order of liturgical usage), about eight thousand Latin manuscripts, more than one thousand manuscripts in other ancient versions such as Syriac and Coptic, and thousands of quotations—virtually the whole New Testament—in citations by the various early church fathers. The actual amount of substantive variation among these many manuscripts is very small. F. F. Bruce summarizes, "The variant readings about which any doubt remains among textual critics of the New Testament affect no material question of historic fact or of Christian faith and practice."[4]

Historical reliability

Unlike the sacred texts of most other religions, the Bible is replete with historical references, and therefore is amenable to cross-checking with other historical sources. Numerous examples have been brought forward to allegedly demonstrate the historical inaccuracy of Scripture, and time and again these claims have been disproved as ancient historical records have come to light. In the nineteenth century, it was frequently claimed, for example, that the Hittite nation, mentioned often in the Old Testament, never existed; but the extensive Hittite Empire has subsequently been uncovered in modern-day Turkey.[5] Until a few years ago, scholars continued to insist that camels were not domesticated until long after the time of Abraham, thus rendering the accounts of camels among the herds of the patriarchs as anachronistic; but extensive evidence has recently appeared for the early domestication of camels.[6] Historical evidence has also appeared that confirms the accuracy of various other aspects of domestic life among the patriarchs, which had been challenged (see the Mari and Nuzi tablets).[7] The existence of the Babylonian king Belshazzar was long questioned by critical scholars, despite his mention in the book of Daniel; but many details of his life and reign have since appeared in historical records.[8] Scholars long considered the chronology of the Hebrew kings as hopelessly muddled and inaccurate, but the work of Edwin Thiele and others has demonstrated the amazing reliability and consistency of the chronology in the books of Kings and Chronicles.[9]

The world-renowned Egyptologist Kenneth A. Kitchen devoted a large part of his scholarly career to comparing the historical data of Scripture with other ancient Near Eastern records. In his magnum opus, *On the Reliability of the Old Testament,* he details his findings. His conclusion is straightforward: "We have a consistent level of good, fact-based correlations right through from circa 2000 B.C. (with earlier roots) down to 400 B.C. In terms of general reliability—and much more could have been instanced than there was room for here—the Old Testament comes out remarkably well, so long as its writings and writers are treated fairly and evenhandedly, in line with independent data, open to all."[10]

The same can be said regarding the New Testament. Paul Barnett, in his comprehensive volume *Is the New Testament Reliable?* summarizes numerous ways "in which we are able to objectively crosscheck historical data from source to source with respect to Jesus and Christian origins. . . . At many points of historical importance about Jesus and Christian beginnings we have not one but several independent sources, not all of them sympathetic to Jesus. If we accept the historicity of the Jewish War on the grounds of independent sources that are able to be crosschecked it is inconsistent to doubt the essential historicity of Jesus and the early church."[11]

Unlike much of the ancient Near Eastern and Greco-Roman propaganda writing of history, as in the historical annals of the major world empires, where no defeats or personal faults of the kings are recorded, the biblical records do not gloss over Israel's defeats in battle nor the moral faults of its historical figures. We have numerous occasions mentioned in Scripture when Israel failed to trust in God and suffered defeat at the hands of their enemies. With regard to prominent individuals in the covenant line, we find, for example, a record of Jacob's deception of his father and stealing his brother's birthright (Genesis 27) and of King David's sins of adultery and murder against Bathsheba and Uriah, respectively (2 Samuel 11; 12). Biblical history is thus actually *more* "true to life" than the historical writings of surrounding nations.

Prophetic reliability

What most distinctly sets Scripture apart from the sacred texts of other religions, and from all other ancient literature, is its claim to accurately predict the distant future. Out of the entire Bible's 31,124 verses, 8,352 verses contain predictive material, about 27 percent of the total.[12] The prophet Isaiah challenged the so-called gods of the ancient Near East to prove their existence by their ability to tell the future: "Tell us what the future holds, so we may know that you are gods" (Isaiah 41:23; cf. 45:21; 46:10). Jesus likewise emphasized fulfilled prophecy as an evidence of the truthfulness of His claims: "I have told you now before it happens, so that when it does happen you will believe" (John 14:29).

Another chapter of this book will address predictive prophecy in more detail, but here we sample some of the Bible's amazingly accurate predictions of future events.[13] Already in the time of Moses, God predicted that the Messiah would come from the tribe of Judah (Genesis 49:10). Later Old Testament prophets predicted His virgin birth (Isaiah 7:14), the place of His birth in Bethlehem (Micah 5:2), and His growing up in Galilee (Isaiah 9:1, 2). The book of Daniel records the angel Gabriel's prediction of the exact time of Christ's coming as the "Anointed One," in the seventy-weeks-of-years prophecy (Daniel 9:24–27), starting with Artaxerxes's decree in 457 B.C. to rebuild Jerusalem, and being fulfilled when Christ was anointed by the Holy Spirit at His baptism in A.D. 27. In this prophecy Christ's death is also predicted to occur in the midst of that last week-of-years, A.D. 31.

Daniel's prophecies of the sixth century B.C. also foretold the exact course of world history, with the world empires coming in succession just as shown in vision: Babylon, Medo-Persia, Greece, Rome (Daniel 2; 7; 8), and the divided kingdoms. Jeremiah predicted the seventy years of Judah's Babylonian captivity (Jeremiah 29:10). Isaiah foretold a century in advance—by name!—the rise of Cyrus, king of the Persians, his troops' conquering of Babylon by diverting the waters of the Euphrates River, and Cyrus's decree that would allow the Israelite captives to return to their homeland (Isaiah 44:24–28; 45:1, 13). Ezekiel predicted the fall of the city of Tyre, giving details that would have been impossible to know in advance: the mainland (old city) destroyed by Nebuchadnezzar, another nation (Alexander and the Greeks) coming later against the (new, island) city, scraping the old site bare as a flat rock used for the spreading of nets, with debris thrown into the midst of the water, and the kingdom of Tyre never rising again (Ezekiel 26:1–21). It has been calculated that there was one chance in seventy-five million of all these facts concerning the fate of Tyre coming true as predicted.[14] These and many other predictions that have come to pass just as predicted constitute powerful evidence of the Bible's reliability.

Scientific reliability

Although the Bible does not claim to be a textbook on science, statements made by Scripture that deal with issues of cosmology and the phenomena of nature reveal a remarkable reliability and precision, notwithstanding common assertions to the contrary. For example, it has frequently been claimed that the Hebrew word *raqia*, which appears in Genesis 1 and is usually translated as "firmament" in English Bibles, was understood by the ancient Hebrews to be a solid, hemispherical dome or vault resting over a flat disc—the earth. But recent research has shown that this interpretation is based upon a faulty translation of the Babylonian term from which the Hebrew concept was allegedly borrowed. As it now turns out, ancient Mesopotamia had no such concept of a solid heavenly vault, and the Hebrew term *raqia'* does not refer to a solid dome but is best translated as "expanse" or "sky."[15] Furthermore, the Hebrew Bible describes the earth, not as a flat disc, but as spherical in shape and suspended in space without resting upon anything. Isaiah testifies,

> He sits enthroned above the circle [*chug*] of the earth,
> and its people are like grasshoppers.
> He stretches out the heavens like a canopy,
> and spreads them out like a tent to live in (Isaiah 40:22).

The Hebrew word *chug*, often translated as "circle," literally means "sphere." Job declares, "He spreads out the northern skies over empty space; he suspends the earth over nothing" (Job 26:7; cf. 28:25).

The account of Creation in Genesis 1 and 2 has been widely discounted among biblical scholars and scientists in favor of some form of naturalistic evolutionary theory. However, much evidence has been forthcoming in recent years for an alternative paradigm of "intelligent design."[16] Moreover, a growing number of highly educated scientists have chosen to believe in a literal six-day creation of life on earth rather than Darwinian or theistic evolution.[17] Discussions of creation often maintain that Genesis 1 and 2 present two contradictory accounts of origins, and thus these chapters are discounted as historical; but careful analysis reveals that Genesis 1 and 2 are fully complementary accounts.[18] Perhaps the most weighty argument against a recent six-day Creation comes from radiometric dating of earth's rocks that yields very long ages, but a close reading of Genesis 1:1–3 suggests that the unformed-unfilled earth could indeed have been created in deep time (verses 1, 2), while the life on earth was created more recently during the six days of Creation week (verses 3–31).[19]

Biblical passages accurately describe the earth's hydrologic cycle (Job 36:27, 28), global wind currents (Ecclesiastes 1:6, 7), and the sea's currents (Psalm 8:8). Contrary to the consensus of scientists and philosophers in antiquity that the universe was not decaying, the Bible accurately describes the phenomenon of the universe "wear[ing] out like a garment" (Psalm 102:26; Isaiah 51:6; cf. Matthew 24:35). Jeremiah accurately describes the human impossibility of numbering the stars (Jeremiah 33:22). An array of other passages illustrating the Bible's scientific reliability may be cited in areas of hydrology, geology, astronomy, meteorology, biology, and physics.[20]

The Bible is amazingly up-to-date with regard to healthy lifestyle principles. A few examples include the injunction to avoid eating the fat and blood in meat (Genesis 9:4; Leviticus 3:17; 17:10–14); the benefits of a plant-based diet (Genesis 1:29; Daniel 1:10–20); reduction of anxiety and worry in one's lifestyle (Proverbs 12:22; Matthew 6:25–34; Philippians 4:6); the psychosomatic benefit of a cheerful attitude for optimum health (Proverbs 17:22); and the benefit of regularity and simplicity in eating habits (Ecclesiastes 10:17). Biblical legislation from thirty-five hundred years ago also reflects knowledge of hygiene and sanitation and quarantine far in advance of its time (e.g., Deuteronomy 23:12–14; Leviticus 11–15).[21]

Theological and spiritual reliability

Several lines of evidence converge to support the theological and spiritual reliability of the Bible. The remarkable unity and consistency of the Bible's central themes, although composed over a period of fifteen hundred years by more than thirty-five different authors from various walks of life, testifies to the reliability of Scripture's entire theological message (see 2 Peter 1:21).[22]

The exquisite literary artistry of the Bible's poetry and narratives, coupled with the stunningly beautiful literary patterns of the Bible, point toward the truthfulness and reliability of its message, just as in science the truthfulness of a given hypothesis often is ultimately verified by its aesthetic elegance.[23]

The profound depth of theological thought contained in the Bible's great and majestic themes, with mysteries that continually unfold as one searches deeper, are evidence of a great and majestic Divine Author, and thus of its theological reliability (Psalms 92:5; 119:18; Romans 11:33–35).

The moral power of Scripture to change people's lives bears witness to the reliability of its spiritual claims (Hebrews 4:12; John 17:17). Stories of transformed lives, such as that of John Newton, composer of the hymn "Amazing Grace,"[24] may be combined with the accounts of the constancy of martyrs in holding to Scripture even in the face of death,[25] to give evidence of the reliability of Scripture in its claim to provide transforming spiritual power and sustaining grace through the Spirit of Christ.

The Bible contains more than five thousand promises and specifically invites the reader to claim these promises and prove for oneself its spiritual reliability. Peter testifies, "Through these he has given us his very great and precious promises, so that through them you may participate in the divine nature and escape the corruption in the world caused by evil desires" (2 Peter 1:4). The abundance of personal testimonies as to God's faithfulness in fulfilling His promises to those who claim them constitutes powerful evidence of the reliability of the spiritual claims of Scripture.[26]

The ultimate proof of the Bible's reliability: Personal experience and the inner witness of the Holy Spirit

John Calvin has rightly pointed out that all of the various kinds of evidence ("proofs") for Scripture's reliability (such as summarized above) are only of relative value, and are helpful only in light of the ultimate evidence: the inner witness of the Spirit. He writes,

> The testimony of the Spirit is superior to reason. For as God alone can properly bear witness to his own words, so these words will not obtain full credit in the hearts of men, until they are sealed by the inward testimony of the Spirit.[27]

> In vain were the authority of Scripture fortified by argument, or supported by the consent of the Church, or confirmed by any other helps, if unaccompanied by an assurance higher and stronger than human judgment can give. Till this better foundation has been laid, the authority of Scripture remains in suspense.[28]

The Bible invites us to "taste and see that the LORD is good" (Psalm 34:8), and promises that "faith comes by hearing, and hearing by the word of God" (Romans 10:17, NKJV). I have personally "tasted" God's Word. I have claimed many of the Bible's thousands of promises relating both to spiritual and temporal needs (e.g., Psalm 119:9, 11, 104; Proverbs 3:5, 6; John 16:13; Philippians 4:6, 7; James 1:5), and found that God is faithful in fulfilling His Word. I have come to trust the Person behind the Book, the Living Word behind His Written Word (John 1:1; Revelation 19:13). While the other evidences of the Bible's reliability have had their due weight in my thinking, it was the inner witness of the Spirit that brought the settled conviction that Scripture is fully reliable (John 3:33; Romans

8:16; 1 John 5:6). I have found true in my own experience what Ellen White describes, " 'Why do I believe the Bible? Because I have found it to be the voice of God to my soul.' We may have the witness in ourselves that the Bible is true."[29] I invite the reader to "taste" and see that the God of Scripture is trustworthy and good, and be open to receive the inner testimony of the Spirit that Scripture is indeed the utterly reliable Word of God!

For further reading:

Lutzer, Erwin W. *Seven Reasons Why You Can Trust the Bible.* Chicago: Moody, 1998.

MacArthur, John, Jr. *You Can Trust the Bible.* Chicago: Moody, 1988.

McDowell, Josh. *Evidence That Demands a Verdict: Historical Evidences for the Christian Faith.* San Bernardino, Calif.: Campus Crusade for Christ International, 1972.

———. *More Evidence That Demands a Verdict: Historical Evidences for the Christian Scriptures.* San Bernardino, Calif.: Campus Crusade for Christ International, 1975.

Muncaster, Ralph O. *Can You Trust the Bible?* Eugene, Ore.: Harvest House, 2000.

Richard M. Davidson *pastored in Arizona for a few years before going to the Theological Seminary at Andrews University. There he obtained his PhD in the Old Testament in 1980 and has remained. During these years, he has taught hundreds of seminary students and was for twenty-five years chair of the Old Testament Department. His influence has gone beyond the classroom through his writings, including the books* A Love Song for the Sabbath *and* Flame of Yahweh: Sexuality in the Old Testament. *He has authored many papers and articles, both for general and learned publics. He has made presentations at learned societies and*

Seventh-day Adventist Church gatherings in the United States, Europe, Asia, and Latin America. Even as he carries out professional duties, he is active in his local Adventist congregation in Eau Claire, Michigan. His wife, Jo Ann Davidson, is author of one of the chapters of this book.

References

[1] Richard M. Davidson, "Biblical Interpretation," in *Handbook of Seventh-day Adventist Theology*, ed. Raoul Dederen (Hagerstown, Md.: Review and Herald® Publishing Association, 2000), 63. All biblical references are to the NIV unless otherwise indicated.

[2] See F. Brown, S. R. Driver, and C. A. Briggs, *A Hebrew and English Lexicon of the Old Testament* (New York: Oxford University Press, 1952; reprinted, Grand Rapids, Mich.: Baker, 1981), 53, 54.

[3] Bruce K. Waltke, "The Textual Criticism of the Old Testament," in *The Expositor's Bible Commentary*, ed. Frank E. Gaebelein (Grand Rapids, Mich.: Zondervan, 1979), 1:214.

[4] F. F. Bruce, *The New Testament Documents: Are They Reliable?* 6th ed. (Grand Rapids, Mich.: Eerdmans, 2003), 14, 15.

[5] Orley Berg, "The Hittites—Fact or Fiction?" in *Treasures in the Sand: What Archaeology Tells Us About the Bible* (Boise, Idaho: Pacific Press® Publishing Association, 1993), 163–168; cf. Ekrem Akurgal, *The Hattian and Hittite Civilizations* (Ankara, Turkey: Republic of Turkey Ministry of Culture, 2001).

[6] Randall W. Younker, "Late Bronze Age Camel Petroglyphs in the Wadi Nasib, Sinai," *Near East Archaeological Society Bulletin* 42 (1997): 47–54.

[7] M. J. Selman, "Comparative Customs and the Patriarchal Age," in *Essays on the Patriarchal Narratives*, eds. A. R. Millard and D. J. Wiseman (Winona Lake, Ind.: Eisenbrauns, 1983), 91–139.

[8] Kenneth A. Kitchen, *On the Reliability of the Old Testament* (Grand Rapids, Mich.: Eerdmans, 2003), 73, 74.

[9] Edwin R. Thiele, *The Mysterious Numbers of the Hebrew Kings,* rev. ed. (Grand Rapids, Mich.: Zondervan, 1983).

[10] Kitchen, *On the Reliability of the Old Testament,* 500.

[11] Paul Barnett, *Is the New Testament Reliable?* 2nd ed. (Downers Grove, Ill.: InterVarsity, 2003), 168, 170.

[12] J. Barton Payne, *Encyclopedia of Biblical Prophecy* (Grand Rapids, Mich.: Baker, 1980), 13.

[13] For a helpful summary of Bible predictions fulfilled in history, see especially Bill Wilson, comp., *The Best of Josh McDowell: A Ready Defense* (Nashville, Tenn.: Thomas Nelson, 1993), 56–73; and John Ankerberg and John Weldon, *A Handbook of Biblical Evidences* (Eugene, Ore.: Harvest House, 1997), 211–257.

[14] Peter W. Stoner, *Science Speaks: An Evaluation of Certain Christian Evidences* (Chicago: Moody, 1963), 80, cited in Wilson, *The Best of Josh McDowell,* 63. Cf. Siegfried H. Horn, *The Spade Confirms the Book,* updated and enlarged ed. (Washington, D.C.: Review and Herald®, 1980), 296–305.

[15] See Randall W. Younker and Richard M. Davidson, "The Myth of the Solid Heavenly Dome" (paper presented at the Seventh-day Adventist Faith and Science Council, Andrews University, October 21, 2009).

[16] See especially William Dembski, *Intelligent Design: The Bridge Between Science and Theology* (Downers Grove, Ill.: InterVarsity, 1999). For a succinct summary of the intelligent design movement and supporting evidence, see Leonard Brand, *Faith, Reason, and Earth History*, 2nd ed. (Berrien Springs, Mich.: Andrews University Press, 2009), 88–107.

[17] See, e.g., John F. Ashton, ed., *In Six Days: Why Fifty Scientists Choose to Believe in Creation* (Sydney: New Holland Publishers, 1999).

[18] Randall W. Younker, "Genesis 2: A Second Creation Account?" in *Creation, Catastrophe, and Calvary*, ed. John T. Baldwin (Hagerstown, Md.: Review and Herald®, 2000), 59–78.

[19] Richard M. Davidson, "The Biblical Account of Origins," *Journal of the Adventist Theological Society* 14 (Spring 2003): 19–25.

[20] A sampling of this evidence is given in Ankerberg and Weldon, *A Handbook of Biblical Evidences*, 339–340. Cf. A. E. Wilder-Smith, *The Reliability of the Bible* (San Diego: Master Books, 1983); and Henry Morris, *The Biblical Basis for Modern Science* (Grand Rapids, Mich.: Baker, 1984).

[21] S. I. McMillen, *None of These Diseases: The Bible's Health Secrets for the 21st Century*, rev. ed. (Grand Rapids, Mich.: Fleming H. Revell, 2000).

[22] See Daniel P. Fuller, *The Unity of the Bible: Unfolding God's Plan for Humanity* (Grand Rapids, Mich.: Zondervan, 1992); and Walter C. Kaiser Jr., *Recovering the Unity of the Bible* (Grand Rapids, Mich.: Zondervan, 2009).

[23] For the aesthetic values of Scripture and their implications for the truthfulness of its message, see especially Jo Ann Davidson, *Toward a Theology of Beauty: A Biblical Perspective* (Lanham: University Press of America, 2008).

[24] Wayne Hooper and Edward E. White, *Companion to the Seventh-day Adventist Hymnal* (Hagerstown, Md.: Review and Herald®, 1988), 159, 652–653.

[25] See, e.g., John Foxe, *Foxe's Book of Martyrs* (Philadelphia: Key, Mielke & Biddle, 1832; reprint, Springdale: Whitaker House, 1981); and Thieleman J. Van Braght, *The Bloody Theatre, or Martyrs' Mirror, of the Defenceless Christians: Who Suffered and Were Put to Death for the Testimony of Jesus, Their Savior, From the Time of Christ Until the Year A.D. 1660*, 1st Eng. ed. (New Lampeter Square, Lancaster County: David Miller, 1837; reprint, Scottdale: Herald Press, 2006).

[26] See, e.g., Glenn A. Coon, *God's Promises Solve My Problems* (Mountain View, Calif.: Pacific Press®, 1979); and Arthur T. Pierson, *George Müller of Bristol* (Westwood: Fleming H. Revell, 1899; reprint, Peabody: Hendrickson, 2008).

[27] John Calvin, *Institutes of the Christian Religion*, trans. Henry Beveridge (Grand Rapids, Mich.: Eerdmans, 1966), 1.7.4 (72).

[28] Calvin, 1.8.1 (74, 75). In book 1, chapter 8 (74–83) Calvin gives thirteen "proofs" of the credibility of Scripture.

[29] Ellen G. White, *Steps to Christ* (Mountain View, Calif.: Pacific Press®, 1956), 112.

JO ANN DAVIDSON

Chapter 2

What Does It Mean to Say That the Bible Is "Inspired"?

Most major religions have what is sometimes referred to as a "sacred text." What Christians call "Holy Scripture" is considered one of these. It is evaluated as the best spiritual literature coming from Christianity and then equated with the writings of Buddha, the Bhagavad Gita of Hinduism, or even the excellent devotional materials by Martin Luther King Jr., or Mother Teresa.

The question needs to be asked, however: are all "sacred texts" alike? Why have Christians insisted on the absolute nature of the Holy Bible? In light of contemporary thinking, we ought to consider once again the primary "textbook" of the Christian faith and its supreme authority for Christians.

Nature of the Bible

First of all, we need to recognize the fundamental assumptions and parameters within which the Bible writers work. Thankfully, these are often stated explicitly. For example, none of the Bible writers ever attempts to prove the existence of God. Without exception, they all assume He exists. Biblical prophets claim to have real knowledge of an Infinite God. They are absolutely certain God speaks through them when they thunder, "Thus says the Lord!"

Moreover, all the Bible writers believe God when He insists that He can foretell the future and that doing so is a mark of His divinity. Isaiah wrote, "Behold, the former things have come to pass, and new things I now declare; before they spring forth I tell you of them" (Isaiah 42:9, RSV). "Indeed before the day was, I am He" (Isaiah 43:13).[1] Through the prophets, God announces the great time prophecies concerning the history of nations and also the coming of the Messiah. Some modern minds assume God cannot be so precise and suggest that the prophecies were written after the fact as predictions. However, this modern attitude of doubting God's ability to predict the future is never found in any of the Bible writers.

Furthermore, Bible writers are absolutely certain that, though infinite, God can and does communicate with human beings. None ever argue that human language is any kind of barrier to direct communication from God. In fact, with great frequency, God is referred to as the actual Person speaking through the prophet. For example, Elijah's words in 1 Kings 21:19 are referred to in 2 Kings 9:25 as the oracle that "the Lord uttered . . . against him" (RSV), and Elijah is not even mentioned.

The work of the prophet

The message of a prophet is always considered equivalent to direct speech from God. Identification of a prophet's words with God's words is so strong in the Old Testament that often we read of God speaking "through" a prophet. And to disobey a prophet's words was to disobey God. In Deuteronomy 18:19, the Lord speaks through Moses of a coming Prophet: "Whoever will not hear My words, which He speaks in My name, I will require it of him."

Bible writers also record numerous incidents of God speaking directly to human beings in the Old Testament, including conversations with Adam and Eve after the Fall (Genesis 1:28–30; 3:9–19) and Job (Job 38–41). There is also the divine call of Abram (Genesis 12:1–3), which was the first of several conversations (including the lengthy conversation in Genesis 18:1–23); later the burning bush dialogue between God and Moses (Exodus 3:1–4:17). The civil code in the Pentateuch is recorded as words spoken directly by God to Moses. The interchange with Elijah at Mount Horeb (1 Kings 19:9–18) is but one of many direct exchanges with the prophets.

Old Testament prophets are consistently pictured as messengers sent by God to speak His words. The repeated use of the introductory formula "thus says the Lord" or its equivalent, used many times, clenches the full authority of a prophetic message. Indeed, a distinguishing characteristic of true prophets throughout the Old Testament is that they do not speak their own words. God said to Jeremiah and Ezekiel: "I have put My words in your mouth" (Jeremiah 1:9); "You shall speak My words to them" (Ezekiel 2:7; cf. 3:27). And those who refused to listen to a prophet were held accountable for refusing to listen to "the words of the Lord which He spoke by the prophet Jeremiah" (Jeremiah 37:2).

Such extensive evidence strongly suggests that biblical prophets experienced something far more than a "divine encounter" that merely implanted mystical conviction and/or admiration for God in their hearts. God's encounters with human beings do not produce glorious feelings but, instead, provide actual information (Deuteronomy 29:29)! Significantly, one Person of the Triune God is known as the *"Word"* (John 1:1; emphasis added).

Closely connected with God speaking are numerous accounts of a prophet writing down the words of God, which are then taken as fully authoritative. A few examples illustrate this: "The Lord said to Moses, 'Write this for a memorial in the book'" (Exodus 17:14). "And Moses wrote all the words of the Lord" (Exodus 24:4). "Joshua wrote these words [statutes, ordinances, and the words of the covenant renewal, Joshua 24:25] in the Book of the Law of God" (verse 26; on Joshua as a prophet, cf. 1 Kings 16:34; Joshua 1; 5; 16–18). "Samuel explained to the people the behavior of royalty, and wrote it in a book and laid it up before the Lord" (1 Samuel 10:25). Even the recording process is divinely controlled with the penman being "moved" or "impelled" (2 Peter 1:21). This written communication thereby has divine authority, as Moses testified, "You shall not add to the word which I command you, nor take from it, that you may keep the commandments of the Lord your God which I command you" (Deuteronomy 4:2).

Revelation and inspiration

Divine revelation or inspiration is never controlled by human beings. It is not a human achievement but a divinely controlled activity. Both Testaments consistently testify that the truth of God is not the end product of a diligent human search for the divine nor somebody's best thoughts about divine matters. It comes exclusively through God's initiative in disclosing Himself. The book of Hebrews gives the word of God divine authority: "Sharper than any two-edged sword, piercing even to the division of soul and spirit, and of joints and marrow, and is a discerner of the thoughts and intents of the heart" (Hebrews 4:12, NIV). A prophet does not speak about God. Rather, God speaks for Himself through His prophets. And human language is assumed to be capable of conveying divine communication.

New Testament writers reflect the same authority as the Old Testament prophets, insisting that they speak by the Holy Spirit (1 Peter 1:10–12), to whom they credit their teaching (1 Corinthians 2:12, 13). Significantly, the same Paul who urges that believers should strive to work together peaceably often uses bold language to defend the absolute truth of the gospel he has preached (Galatians 1:6–9). Apostolic teaching is very directive, issuing commands with absolute authority (1 Thessalonians 4:1, 2; 2 Thessalonians 3:6, 12: "we command" you).

The prophets and apostles do not describe how they recognized the word of God when it came, but it is clear they were certain that God had spoken. Sometimes He spoke in ways that they did not readily understand and, on occasion, even objected to, yet they never questioned the divine origin of the message. However, the Bible was not verbally dictated by God. The human messenger was divinely guided in the selection of apt words to express divine revelation. The individuality of each writer is evident, yet the human and divine elements are virtually inseparable. Ellen White offers intriguing insights: "The Bible, with its God-given truths expressed in the language of men, presents a union of the divine and the human."[2] She further notes that "inspiration acts not on the man's words or his expressions but on the man himself, who, under the influence of the Holy Ghost, is imbued with thoughts. But these words receive the impress of the individual mind. . . . The divine mind and will is combined with the human mind and will; thus the utterances of the man are the word of God."[3]

Continuity and unity of both Testaments

A close reading of the biblical texts reveals a basic continuity and unity of both Testaments. Extensive citations of Old Testament materials in the New Testament indicate that Old Testament writings were considered divine revelation. A few of the many examples include Isaiah's words in Isaiah 7:14, cited as "which was spoken by the Lord through the prophet" (Matthew 1:22). Jesus quotes Genesis 2:24 as words that God said (Matthew 19:5). In quoting what was spoken by the prophet Joel (Joel 2:28–32), Peter inserts "says God," attributing to God the words of Joel (Acts 2:16, 17). Paul and Barnabas quote Isaiah 49:6 as something that "the Lord has commanded us" (Acts 13:47), contending that an Old Testament prophecy placed moral obligation on them also. Paul writes that the Holy Spirit spoke through the prophet Isaiah (Acts 28:25). He also quotes in Romans 9:17 God's speech in Exodus 9:16 as what "Scripture says to the Pharaoh," indicating an equivalence between what Old Testament Scripture says and what God says.

As in the Old Testament, New Testament writers also knew it was possible for God to speak directly to people in human language. Examples include the baptism of Jesus (Matthew 3:17); the Transfiguration (Mark 9:7; Luke 9:35); the conversion of Saul (Acts 9:4); instructions to Ananias (Acts 9:11–16); Peter's vision (Acts 10:13); the revelation to John (Revelation 1:11–3:22). Jesus Himself insisted numerous times that He spoke the words of God. For example, "the Father who sent Me gave Me a command, what I should say and what I should speak" (John 12:49). Paul claimed receiving revelation from God: "If anyone thinks himself to be a prophet or spiritual, let him acknowledge that the things which I write to you are the commandments of the Lord" (1 Corinthians 14:37).

The minds of the New Testament writers are saturated with the Old Testament, quoting it extensively to undergird their theological arguments. The four Gospels make it strikingly obvious that Jesus Christ submitted unreservedly to the Old Testament and confirmed its absolute authority. In His teaching and ethics, it was foundational. Old Testament prophecy was the pattern for His life, as He declared often: "It must be fulfilled" or "as it is written." He didn't rebuke the Jewish theologians of His time for studying the Old Testament but for permitting human tradition to cloud and even falsify God's Written Word (Mark 7:1–13).

Jesus expected everyone to accept the Old Testament as authoritative. Often He would inquire, "Have you not read what David did . . . ? Or have you not read in the law?" (Matthew 12:3–5). When questioned on the issue of divorce, He answered, "Have you not read?" (Matthew 19:4). His response to those upset by children praising loudly in the temple was "Have you never read?" (Matthew 21:16). Once, when being questioned, Jesus told a parable and concluded by questioning, "Have you not read this Scripture?" (Mark 12:10). Responding to a lawyer's question about salvation, Jesus asked, "What is written in the law? What is your reading of it?" (Luke 10:26). The lawyer quoted from the Ten Commandments, and Jesus declared, "You have answered rightly" (verse 28). Asked about last-day events on the Mount of Olives, Jesus urged His questioners to study Daniel (Matthew 24:15).

The apostle Paul continually refers to the Old Testament and insists on its authority. For example, in his letter to the Romans, he makes a powerful argument for the gospel built upon the Old Testament and, in the process, demonstrates the paramount principle of listening to what Scripture says about itself.

Trustworthiness of the Bible

While it is sometimes argued today that the truthfulness of the Bible does not necessarily include historical details, Jesus and the New Testament writers accepted the historicity of the Old Testament. In fact, the New Testament writers use the historical narratives of the Old Testament to undergird the certainty of future actions of God. Israel's history reached its climax in the coming of Jesus. The whole Old Testament was summed up in Him. Paul insists that *all* Scripture has been "given by inspiration of God" (2 Timothy 3:16),[4] not differentiating between different books or sections. The "textbook" Christians hold as the highest authority is self-authenticated in an impressive manner. David Dockery is right: "We must resist relating divine inspiration merely to content and not to form, to the Bible's purpose and not to its essence, or to its thoughts and not to its words. The entirety of Scripture is inspired."[5] This is a crucial point: "Perhaps it has not been stated emphatically enough that *nowhere* in the Old Testament or in the New Testament does any writer give *any* hint of a tendency to distrust or consider slightly unreliable any other part of Scripture. Hundreds of texts encourage God's people to trust Scripture completely, but no text encourages any doubt or even slight mistrust of Scripture."[6]

Contrary to those who today suggest that different portions of Scripture are of questionable value, Ellen White emphatically states,

What Does It Mean to Say That the Bible Is "Inspired"?

What man is there that dares to take that Bible and say this part is inspired and that part is not inspired? I would have both my arms taken off at my shoulders before I would ever make the statement or set my judgment upon the Word of God as to what is inspired and what is not inspired. . . .

. . . Never let mortal man sit in judgment upon the Word of God or pass sentence as to how much of this is inspired and how much is not inspired, and that this is more inspired than some other portions. God warns him off that ground. God has not given him any such work to do. . . .

We call on you to take your Bible, but do not put a sacrilegious hand upon it, and say, "That is not inspired," simply because somebody else has said so. Not a jot or tittle is ever to be taken from that Word. Hands off, brethren! Do not touch the ark.[7]

God Himself expresses the same sentiment:

Thus says the LORD:
"Heaven is My throne,
And earth is My footstool.
Where is the house that you will build Me?
And where is the place of My rest?
For all those things My hand has made,
And all those things exist,"
says the LORD.
"But on this one will I look:

On him who is poor and of a contrite spirit,
And who trembles at My word" (Isaiah 66:1, 2).

The Christian doctrine of Scripture is about a Book. But really, it is more than a Book. The Bible confronts us with a God who yearns for His children, who is in earnest to communicate His love to them, and who ultimately loves them more than He loved His own life. Fleming Rutledge expresses my sentiments eloquently: "Every time I think I am losing my faith, the Biblical story seizes me yet again with a life all its own. No other religious document has this power. I remain convinced in spite of all the arguments that God really does inhabit this text. . . . The God we proclaim to you today is not the 'vague abstraction' of the philosophers or the 'insubstantial shadow' of the New Agers. . . . He is the living God."[8]

Jo Ann Davidson is the daughter of missionary parents, and is a fourth generation Seventh-day Adventist. Formerly a homeschooling mother and music instructor, she now teaches in the Andrews University Theological Seminary—the first woman to teach in the theology department. She earned her PhD in systematic theology from Trinity Evangelical Divinity School in 2000. Her articles have appeared in the Adventist Review, Signs of the Times®, *and the* Journal of the Adventist Theological Society. *Her column, "Let's Face It," which has a woman's slant on theology, appears regularly in the journal* Perspective Digest. *She has also authored the books* Jonah: The Inside Story, Glimpses of Our God, *and* Toward a Theology of Beauty: A Biblical Perspective. *She finds great fulfillment in her many roles as wife, mother, daughter, sister, auntie, teacher, musician, student, and Seventh-day Adventist Christian.*

References

[1] Unless otherwise noted, all Bible quotations are from the New King James Version.

[2] Ellen G. White, *The Great Controversy* (Mountain View, Calif.: Pacific Press®, 1911), vi.

[3] White, *Selected Messages,* bk. 1 (Washington, D.C.: Review and Herald®, 1958), 21.

[4] The Greek text reads *theopneustos,* "God breathed."

[5] David S. Dockery, *Christian Scripture: An Evangelical Perspective on Inspiration, Authority and Interpretation* (Nashville, Tenn.: Broadman and Holman, 1995), 40.

[6] Wayne A. Grudem, "Scripture's Self-Attestation and the Problem of Formulating a Doctrine of Scripture," in *Scripture and Truth,* eds. D. A. Carson and John D. Woodbridge (Grand Rapids, Mich.: Baker Books, 1992), 58, 59; emphasis Grudem's.

[7] White, cited in "Ellen G. White Comments," *Seventh-day Adventist Bible Commentary,* vol. 7 (Washington, D.C.: Review and Herald®, 1957), 919, 920.

[8] Fleming Rutledge, *Help My Unbelief* (Grand Rapids, Mich.: Eerdmans, 2000), 25.

RANDALL W. YOUNKER

Chapter 3

To What Extent Do Archaeological Discoveries Confirm the Bible?

A little over ten years ago, the Public Broadcasting Service network (PBS) aired a critically acclaimed special on Genesis. While the program received numerous favorable reviews, a question that apparently lurked in the back of many minds was openly voiced in the October 20, 1996, *Newsweek* article: "But Did It Really Happen?" The cover of the October 25, 1999, issue of *U.S. News & World Report* displayed a painting depicting Eve offering Adam an apple, under which was the query "Is the Bible True?" Both of these major newsmagazines point to a question (a modernist question, if you will) that continues to gnaw at people today—is the Bible true?

Why does this question continue to haunt contemporary society? It is one thing to read and even enjoy the stories in the Bible; it is quite another to believe that they actually happened. If God actually entered into history through our space-time continuum—if the Bible stories are true and the claims that the Bible makes are real (e.g., Jesus is indeed returning to earth as Judge and Redeemer)—that would also mean that humans have certain moral obligations to God and their fellow humans!

Importance of biblical history to faith

Both evangelical Christian philosopher Ronald Nash[1] and theologian Gerhard Maier[2] acknowledge that faith, and the personal relationship with God that it encompasses, is impossible without history. This is because (as they argue) it is in historical events (both past and present) that we encounter God, come to know Him, and develop a personal relationship with Him. After supporting this with several scriptural examples, Maier comments, "Faith can only arise where God has previously—not thought, but acted. That is, it arises as biblical faith only in the realm of biblical revelation whose occurrence has extended itself into history."[3]

The evangelical scholar Carl F. H. Henry points out that "God reveals himself . . . within this external history in unique saving acts."[4] Therefore, Gerhard Maier adds, we must insist that "historical acts" belong inextricably to divine revelation,

> God is the ultimate ground of history. God revealed himself in history in such a way that his revelation could be discerned even in the midst of a fallen human race. When we speak of the historical nature of the Bible, we have in mind precisely that crossover of the eternal divine revelation into the present space-time world (*transitio revelationis*).[5]

Significantly, Maier is careful to note that historical investigation alone cannot create faith, because faith requires a personal relationship with the One God who encounters us in the events of history. This encounter with God is not simply knowledge or persuasion on the intellectual level that God exists—many may believe in God's existence but are not believers and will not be saved.

This is, in part, why believers are (or should be) reluctant to say that history (or archaeology) "proves" faith. By itself, it can't. Nevertheless, history plays a crucial role because genuine interpersonal knowledge is impossible apart from historical knowledge. As Nash points out,

> To whatever extent faith knowledge is analogous to interpersonal knowledge, it is obvious that a faith commitment requires prior historical knowledge. Trust is inseparable from knowledge. When a person becomes a friend or falls in love he makes a commitment that goes beyond what he knows; but nonetheless the commitment would never have been made without some prior knowledge. The person making the commitment reasons that even though there may be much about this person he does not know, he knows enough to believe, to trust, to make a commitment that goes beyond the evidence. But the commitment is still based on some evidence.[6]

Moreover, cognitive knowledge continues to be important, even essential, to interpersonal knowledge; *historical* knowledge continues to be relevant even after a personal commitment is made.[7]

What archaeology can not and can do

Archaeology, of course, is a scientific way of "resurrecting" history. Thus, its relevancy in exploring biblical history seems obvious. However, there are a few things that archaeology cannot or should not do. For example, archaeology should not be considered a final authority with regard to biblical veracity. That is to say, archaeology's purpose cannot be to prove the Bible. If we allow archaeology that position of authority, we have subjugated the Bible's own self-described authority to one outside of the text. Moreover, as Adventist archaeologist and Old Testament scholar Lloyd Willis notes, "Because archaeology is interpretive in nature [subjective] apparent contradictions are inevitable, and the Christian can then be left in a quandary. Faith should be in God and Scripture."[8] There are some other inherent weaknesses in archaeology that also make it unsuitable to serve as an absolute authority. It cannot generally prove the details of historically significant events, nor can it verify the theological dimensions of biblical events. For these and other reasons, archaeology does not provide a suitable foundation for faith.

Positive contributions of archaeology

In spite of these limitations, however, archaeology can do a number of positive things with regards to the Bible. For example, it can serve as a test for reconstructions of the biblical texts made by historical critics. That is to say, archaeology can "falsify" bad theories about the Bible or, to put it in a more positive light, archaeology can provide a different point of view "against which to test . . . [a historical-critical] interpretation of the documents."[9] Second, archaeology can provide the contemporary setting and context—historical, cultural, linguistic, and religious—for the writing of biblical materials and the events these materials describe. In this sense, it can sometimes provide clarification. Third, it can, at times, offer corroborative evidence for the existence of specific people, places, and even events mentioned in the biblical writings.

The positive contributions of archaeology may not be essential for the believer, although they can be edifying for an already established faith. However, archaeology can help the unbeliever who is challenged by claims that the events and people of the Bible are totally fictitious. Of course, archaeological data cannot in themselves result in conversion—only the Holy Spirit can do that—but it can provide information that the Holy Spirit can use to positively impress a struggling individual.

Archaeology, biblical people, and events

It might be interesting and useful to see examples of the positive contributions of archaeology to the understanding of biblical history. From the very beginnings of modern explorations into the ancient Near East, archaeology has continuously verified the existence of people mentioned in the Bible as well as the occurrence of biblical events. The first of these discoveries that has a direct bearing on the Bible was made in 1843, by Paul Emile Botta (1802–1870), a French consular officer and antiquarian. He was excavating at Khorsabad, also known as Dur Sharrukin (Sargon's Castle), in Iraq. He found a number of cuneiform tablets as well as bas-reliefs with inscriptions. When he brought these back to Europe, a scholar named Longperrier was able to make out the name *Sar-gin* on one of the inscriptions. He was able to identify this name with Sargon, the king of Assyria mentioned in Isaiah 20:1. This was, to my knowledge, the first biblical character whose existence was confirmed independently of the Bible.

In 1846, an Irish clergyman named Edward Hincks was able to read the name of King Nebuchadnezzar (II) and his father on clay bricks that travelers had brought back from Mesopotamia. This confirmed the existence of this person noted in the book of Daniel, as well as his claim to be a great builder of Babylon.

To What Extent Do Archaeological Discoveries Confirm the Bible?

About this same time, British archaeologist Austen Henry Layard was excavating the twin sites of Kuyunjik and Nebi Yunus (traditional site of Jonah's grave), both of which turned out to be part of biblical Nineveh.[10] Among the biblically significant finds uncovered by Layard was the Black Obelisk (1846). On it scholars were able to identify the names of people mentioned in the Bible: Shalmaneser (III), the same person mentioned in 2 Kings 17:13, and Jehu, son of the house of Omri. Jehu, of course, was the king of Israel known for his aggressive chariot driving (2 Kings 9:20). By 1853, Layard, with the help of his epigraphers, was able to claim that he had found nearly fifty-five rulers, cities, and countries mentioned in both the Old Testament and the newly discovered Assyrian texts.[11]

While many additional finds were made between 1850 and 1990, some of the recent discoveries have been equally exciting. These include the probable ossuary of Caiaphas, the high priest who presided over part of Jesus' trial; the discovery of King David's name on an Aramaic stele from Tel Dan; the name of Baruch, Jeremiah's scribe (as well as his fingerprint); and the seal of King Hezekiah.

Historical, cultural, linguistic, and religious settings and context

Archaeology has provided dramatic historic, cultural, linguistic, and religious insights into the fall of Lachish, recounted in 2 Kings 18. Not only do we have the biblical account, but Sennacherib's pictorial account has been recovered from his palace, as well as his own written account of the battle. In addition to this, the site of Lachish has been excavated, bringing to light even more details of the battle. These discoveries have informed us of all sorts of details about this biblical event.

Refuting criticisms against the Bible's historicity

The final area where archaeology can make a contribution is in refuting the challenges that critics have laid against the Bible's historical veracity. For example, during the latter part of the nineteenth century, when the historical-critical method was becoming widely accepted, a favorite example presented as illustrating the Bible's historical inaccuracy was the references in Daniel to Belshazzar as the final king of Babylon. Some scholars, such as Ferdinand Hitzig in his commentary on Daniel,[12] went so far as to suggest that Belshazzar was a pure invention on the part of the writer of Daniel chapter 5. However, as is now well known, in 1854 some clay cylinders were found at the ancient city of Ur, upon one of which was inscribed a prayer on behalf of King Nabonidus and his son—Belshazzar. Other documents were subsequently discovered that indicate that King Nabonidus preferred to live in Teima in northern Arabia rather than in the capital city of Babylon. He apparently left his son Belshazzar in charge—in effect a coregent—as second in the kingdom. This position assigned to Belshazzar explains why he offered Daniel the third highest position in the land instead of the second, which Belshazzar already occupied.

The point here, however, is not to show how archaeology has proven the Bible. Indeed, none of these Belshazzar tablets actually refers to those final, fateful events in the great hall of the palace that Daniel describes, where the king was weighed in the balances and found wanting. In this case, archaeology is more effective in disproving the critic's claims that there was no Belshazzar than in proving the Bible account of events as true. The archaeological evidence that there was indeed such an individual is gratifying to the believer, but is not and should not be necessary in proving the historicity of the Bible.

Another objection of critics is the apparent presence of anachronisms in the Bible. By anachronism we refer to an event or phenomenon from a later period of history being read into an earlier period. Some good examples of this include the references in the patriarchal narratives to camels and tents (Genesis 12:16). It was argued that camels were not domesticated until well into the first millennium B.C., well after the supposed patriarchal period in the second millennium. Similarly, it was argued that tent dwelling (as in the story of Abraham and his family) was more common in the first millennium than the second. The references to tents and to camels were, therefore, anachronistic, and cast doubt upon the historical reliability of the Genesis narratives that contained them.

My own research into domesticated camels has shown the critics to be wrong. For example, during an excursion into the Wadi Nasib in the Sinai in July 1998, I noticed a petroglyph of a camel being led by a man not far from a stele of Ammenemes III and some proto-Sinaitic (early alphabetic) inscriptions. Based on the patina of the petroglyphs and the dates of the accompanying inscriptions and nearby archaeological remains, this camel petroglyph dates to the Late Bronze Age, probably not later than 1500 B.C.[13] Clearly, scholars who have denied the presence of domesticated camels in the second millennium B.C. have been committing the fallacy of arguing from silence. This approach should not be allowed to cast doubt upon the veracity of any historical document, let alone Scripture.

Conclusion

In summary, we have attempted to describe the relationship of archaeology with the study of Scripture within a context that accepts the Bible as the fully inspired, authoritative Word of God. This view affirms that the Bible provides a truthful and accurate history of God's dealings with humanity from the time of Creation to the present age. Because the God of the Bible is the Source of truth and justice, He invites us to test Him and to investigate His claims. This can be done through a number of disciplines, including archaeology. Scripture reminds us that the God of the Bible has crossed into our space-time continuum, into our history. He has done this through His Word, through His Son, and through the events of history. Thus, through history, we can meet God, and because He is in charge of history, it can best be understood when the investigator is in a relationship with God. There can, therefore, be no genuine objective historical investigation apart from contact with God. Moreover, because the Bible is a revelation from God, who informs us that what He has revealed is true, Bible-believing archaeologists do not use their discipline to test the authenticity of Scripture's claims—archaeology does not stand in judgment of Scripture. However, it can be profitably used to clarify and corroborate the statements of Scripture; it can be used to edify believers; and it can be used to show the shortcomings of historical reconstructions that are in conflict with the claims of Scripture. Ultimately, its goal should be to bring humanity into a closer understanding of God and a saving relationship with the Creator.

For further reading:
The Archaeological Study Bible. Grand Rapids, Mich.: Zondervan, 2005.
Hoffmeier, James K. *Israel in Egypt: The Evidence for the Authenticity of the Exodus Tradition.* New York: Oxford University Press, 1999.
Kitchen, Kenneth A. *On the Reliability of the Old Testament.* Grand Rapids, Mich.: Eerdmans, 2003.

Provan, Iain, V. Philips Long, and Tremper Longman III. *A Biblical History of Israel.* Louisville, Ky.: Westminster John Knox, 2003.

Randall W. Younker *holds BA and MA degrees in religion and biology from Pacific Union College and an MA and a PhD in Near Eastern Archaeology from the University of Arizona. He serves as professor of Old Testament and Biblical Archaeology at the Seventh-day Adventist Theological Seminary of Andrews University, where he is also the director of the Institute of Archaeology and the Siegfried Horn Museum. He has directed numerous interdisciplinary seasons of archaeological field research in Israel and Jordan and is a trustee of the American Schools of Oriental Research. He has coedited seven books, and published scores of scholarly articles.*

References

[1] Ronald Nash, *Christian Faith and Historical Understanding* (Grand Rapids, Mich.: Zondervan, 1984).

[2] Gerhard Maier, *Biblical Hermeneutics,* trans. R. W. Yarbrough (Wheaton, Ill.: Crossway, 1994).

[3] Ibid., 219.

[4] C. F. H. Henry, *Revelation and Authority* (Waco, Tex.: Word Books, 1976), 11.

[5] Maier, *Biblical Hermeneutics,* 210.

[6] Nash, *Christian Faith and Historical Understanding,* 149.

[7] Ibid.

[8] Lloyd A. Willis, *Archaeology in Adventist Literature: 1937–1980* (Berrien Springs, Mich.: Andrews University Press, 1982), 560n1.

[9] H. Darrell Lance, *The Old Testament and the Archaeologist* (Philadelphia, Pa.: Fortress Press, 1981), 66.

[10] Austen H. Layard, *Discoveries in the Ruins of Nineveh and Babylon* (London: John Murray, 1883).

[11] P. R. S. Moorey, *A Century of Biblical Archaeology* (Louisville, Ky.: Westminster John Knox Press, 1991), 11.

[12] F. Hitzig, *Das Buch Daniel* (Leipzig: Weidmann, 1850), 75.

[13] Randall W. Younker, "Late Bronze Age Camel Petroglyphs in the Wadi Nasib, Sinai," *Near East Archaeological Society Bulletin* 42 (1977): 47–54.

CLIFFORD GOLDSTEIN

Chapter 4

Why Do I Believe in God?

*And yet I'm sitting by this river, that's a fact.
And since I am here
I must have come from somewhere.*
—Wisława Szymborska[1]

Behind the bare phenomenal facts, as my tough-minded old friend Chauncey Wright, the great Harvard empiricist of my youth, used to say, there is nothing.
—William James[2]

C. S. Lewis wrote about an acquaintance, "the hardest boiled of all the atheists I ever knew,"[3] the "cynics of cynics, the toughest of the toughs"[4] when it came to faith, yet who said to Lewis that "the historicity of the Gospels was really surprisingly good."[5] Still agnostic, Lewis was floored. If the Gospels were historically accurate, then miracles occurred; and, if miracles occurred, then his own atheistic, materialistic *Weltanschauung* was, simply, wrong.

I use this account, not as an intro into a gospel apologetic, but as an intro into what has represented, from antiquity, the two mothers of all metanarratives: the *a priori* materialistic, atheistic worldview, held by the pre-Socratic atomists up through the radical wing of the *philosophes* and, today, most loudly proclaimed by the New Atheists; in contrast, of course, is belief in some type of supernatural being(s), from Zoroaster's Ahura Mazda to Voltaire's deism to Calvinist predestinarianism (and everything else as well). Either metanarrative (any version), Lewis knew, negated the other.

This paper, as the title unsubtly suggests, defends the latter.

Credo ut intelligam

One case for the existence of God was proposed by Anselm (c. 1033–1109). In its simplest form (more sophisticated versions exist), the ontological argument goes like this: God is that which no greater can be conceived. For something to be that which nothing greater can be conceived means it would have to exist, because what exists is greater than what does not. Hence, God exists.

Probably because that move isn't likely to transition anyone from atheism to what Christians call "the new birth," Anselm also coined the famous phrase *Credo ut intelligam* ("I believe in order that I may understand"). Arguments in favor of God's existence tend to be more effective *after* one already believes, which might have been Anselm's point with the ontological argument to begin with: not to prove the existence of God but, rather, to start with belief and then work backwards in order to defend and understand it.

That's the approach of my paper. The title, "Why Do I Believe in

God?" implies, *a priori,* a different approach than were it titled "Why God Exists." The former automatically injects a personal, subjective element, even an experiential one (essential, perhaps, for belief in God anyway). A personal subjective element doesn't denude an argument of truth any more than a personal dislike of cylindrical space makes Riemannian geometry false. Besides, if this paper were titled "Why Do I Believe God Doesn't Exist?" who believes the subjective element wouldn't be pervasive there, either?

Something like "nothing"

Why do I believe in God? Why do I believe in *anything*? Why is there anything at all to believe in, or even a subjective consciousness such as myself to believe in it? As Leibniz and others have famously asked, *Why is there something instead of nothing?*

The answer, obviously, must be found in some version of the above-mentioned metanarratives (you can't get more "meta" than creation). The universe originated either through natural or through supernatural origins. If the latter, the universe was made by a being (or beings) greater than, and prior to, it. Otherwise, creation had to have occurred naturally, out of itself. This leads to the question: how did it first get there in order to arise out of itself? The only apparent out is an eternal universe, one that always existed, a concept that leads to a difficult paradox. Known as the Kalām cosmological argument, it states that an infinitely old universe is impossible because it would imply that an infinite amount of time must have been passed in order to have reached this (or any present) moment. But how could an infinite amount of time (or, for that matter, of anything) have ever been completed? In other words, if the universe existed infinitely in the past, then an infinite number of moments must have been traversed in order to get where we are now. But if we can't count, even in our heads, to infinity, how could in reality an infinite number of *moments* have been completed?

Whatever the validity (or weakness) of that argument, big bang cosmogony has all but mooted it, anyway. The universe, once not existing, came into existence. Though cosmologists, working backward, speculate about the first millionth of a second and so forth of the universe's nascence, the implications of it having one were scientifically, and metaphysically, revolutionary.

That idea, that the universe had a beginning, helped convince "the world's most notorious atheist,"[6] Antony Flew, of the existence of a Creator. Though he had simply taken "the universe and its most fundamental features as the ultimate fact,"[7] he no longer could, not in the face of big bang cosmogony. Meanwhile, finding the argument *du jour* that "nothing" created the universe less than satisfactory, Flew came to believe in some sort of, as he put it, "divine mind."[8] (Bill Bryson's assertion—"It seems impossible that you could get something from nothing, but the fact that once there was nothing but now there is a universe is evident proof that you can"[9]—is as ludicrous as it sounds.)

This argument is, of course, nothing new. It just has the benefit of common sense, and now a little astrophysics to boot. It's not an algebraic proof of God's existence, never has been. It's just that when "nothing"— that which, by definition, does not exist—is posited instead of God as the creative force behind cosmic origins, one has to wonder about the logic of those looking for something, anything, even *nothing*, as opposed to God as the Source of our existence. God, the foundation of all existence, is replaced by "nothing," the negation of all existence? Perhaps Tennyson's line, "Believing where we cannot prove," though aimed at Christian believers, missed its target completely?

Stephen Hawking's brain

Despite pronouncements of its death in 1779, after a long and distinguished history, the teleological argument rages today. "David Hume effectively demolished," wrote Terrence W. Tilley, "the modern argument from design in his *Dialogues Concerning Natural Religion* (1779)."[10] Hume did no such thing. He articulately revealed the *limits* of the argument, but, big deal. What nondeductive argument doesn't have limits? Design is an inference, not a proof.

Though conceding (through the mouth of a person engaged in a dialogue) an intricacy and design in nature "to a degree beyond what human senses and faculties can trace or explain"[11] (this was written in the era of the "simple cell," the Pleistocene in terms of biological science), Hume dismissed the idea of a Creator behind it all. Ultimately, though, he had to argue that "matter may contain the source or spring of order originally, within itself, . . . that the several elements, from an internal unknown cause, may fall into the most exquisite arrangement."[12]

Hume's *Dialogues* simply pushed the argument back, nothing more. Where did matter get the information and ability to organize itself into this "exquisite arrangement" (which, compared to what we know today, would appear crude)? It's easier to imagine paper and ink, from something inherent in themselves, creating Tolstoy's *War and Peace*, than to imagine carbon, water, and proteins organizing themselves into a single cell, much less the processes that led to Stephen Hawking's brain.

Science has supposedly given the answer to how carbon, water, and proteins led to that brain: random mutation and natural selection, of course. Though this isn't the place to debate neo-Darwinianism, in regards to the question of God's existence, science has become a two-edged sword, with the sharpest edge cutting against atheistic evolution. While the science about how, or even if, random mutation and natural selection could have created the complexity of life is contentiously debated, what isn't contentious, or debated, is the complexity itself.

The irony shouldn't be missed: the more complexity science finds in life, the less likely that the means science claims for its origins becomes. Such complexity was another factor that helped convert Antony Flew, who quoted Nobel Prize-winning physiologist, George Wald: "We choose to believe the impossible: that life arose spontaneously by chance."[13]

Not so ready to concede the impossible, some postulate the improbable instead. Admitting that the complexity of life makes its chance origins in our universe unlikely ("impossible"), some cosmologists have argued that there are many universes, perhaps even an infinite number, which means that the chances of one (ours) accidentally being *biophilic*, friendly to life, greatly increases. Who needs even one God when an infinite number of universes (of which there is not the slightest proof of more than one) will do it instead? And, even if one accepted the multiverse theory, it only pushes the argument back, as did Hume. An infinite number of universes simply makes the question of their origin *infinitely* more pressing than does the existence of one.

Look at the extremes here: life arose from "nothing," or from one of an infinite number of universes. Wouldn't a supernatural Creator be a more reasonable explanation than either of the others?

Richard Dawkins, of course, will have none of it. Amid all the hype surrounding *The God Delusion,* his attack on the teleological argument, at least metaphysically, was surprisingly puerile. One motif echoes through the philippic: who created God? "A designer God," he asserted, "cannot be used to explain organized complexity because any God capable of designing anything would have to be complex enough to demand the same kind of explanation in his own right."[14] But God, an eternal God, by definition, doesn't have a Creator, He *is* the Creator; a caused universe, and all that's in it, in contrast, does. So confined by naturalism, Dawkins can't understand the qualitative difference between the made and the maker. *Guernica,* not Picasso, needed a painter (I said, "painter," not Creator, a subtle but crucial difference).

Everything, from cell membrane physiology to grapefruit to human sexuality, makes God so much more likely as the explanation for their functionality, beauty, and purpose than does any explanation predicated on a chance confluence of particles and forces that, in and of themselves, require a sufficient cause outside of, greater than, and anterior to them.

Besides, what is more likely to have been uncaused, anyway—the universe or God?

To demand a miracle

Whatever the Ukrainian proverb ("When you leave the house in Donetsk, bring a knife, in case you run into someone you know") might say about the Donetsk citizenry, it also says something about humanity, which is that we possess moral properties. But how could the constituents of existence (quarks, electrons, color force), all amoral in and of themselves, emerge not only into life, but into consciousness, a consciousness conflicted with moral attributes? The possibility seems absurd. No wonder atheist apologist J. L. Mackie argued that "moral properties constitute so odd a cluster of qualities and relations that are most unlikely to have arisen in the ordinary course of events without an all-powerful god to create them."[15] Mackie solved his problem by denying the properties. Others, not ready for that move, see in those properties evidence for God's existence.

And though the theme of life's meaninglessness in the face of death has been touched on throughout history, in the twentieth century Bryan Magee wrote that, because of death, his life was doomed to nullity, and that "there was no meaning in any of it, no point in any of it; and that in the end, everything was nothing."[16] Yet think about it: the thumb has a purpose, the ear has a purpose, the heart has a purpose, the sun has a purpose—and yet these and untold other "purposes," so finely and majestically woven, culminate into purposelessness? It's like adding positive integers and getting a negative number. If the universe, and all consciousness in it, is doomed to extinction, then our existence has no purpose, a conclusion that contradicts everything about that existence itself, which—from the cellular level outward—screams with purposefulness. No wonder Auden wrote, "Nothing can save us that is possible; we who must die demand a miracle."[17]

And a miracle demands deity, which leads back to Lewis's dilemma. As his atheist friend said, powerful evidence does exist for the historicity of the Gospels, which includes the miracle of Christ's resurrection. Now, just as the discovery of one black swan annuls any worldview that states "all swans are white," even one such miracle annuls any worldview that denies a God who could do them. Of course, proving miracles is another matter, but for those who believe in them, or have experienced the miraculous for themselves, evidence for God's existence becomes lodged, at least partly, in places where—as with music—using logic alone is like applying greasy pliers to a software glitch.

Between the powerful evidence for the resurrection of Jesus, along with biblical prophecies, whose fulfillments alone demand a God as their most logical explanation—prophecies that are, in some cases, rooted in a foundation as firm, as broad, and as unchangeable as world history (such as Daniel 2)—we have been given good reasons for faith. Not foolproof, of course, but so what? Nothing epistemological ever is.

"If we cannot even prove the consistency of arithmetic," wrote physicist John Polkinghorne, "it seems a bit much to hope that God's existence is easier to deal with."[18]

Not easier, perhaps, but manageable all the same.

For further reading:

Craig, William Lane, ed. *Philosophy of Religion: A Reader and a Guide.*
    Piscataway, N.J.: Rutgers University Press, 2002. See specifically Craig.
    "The Kalām Cosmological Argument." 92–113.

Davies, Paul. *Cosmic Jackpot.* New York: Houghton Mifflin, 2007.

Richard, Dennis, ed. *The Book of the Cosmos.* Cambridge: Perseus
    Publishing, 2000.

Wainwright, William J., ed. *The Oxford Handbook of Philosophy of
    Religion.* London: Oxford University Press, 2005.

Wright, N. T. *Surprised by Hope.* New York: Harper Collins, 2008.

Clifford Goldstein *has been editor of the Adult Sabbath School Bible Study Guides since 1999. Previously, he was editor of* Liberty *magazine. From 1983 through 1993, he edited* Shabbat Shalom, *a journal specifically designed for Jewish readers. He obtained a BA at the University of Florida and a MA in ancient Semitic languages at Johns Hopkins University in 1992. He has authored more than twenty books, of which the best known may be* 1844 Made Simple *(1988),* A Pause for Peace *(1992), and* Graffiti in the Holy of Holies *(2003). His latest book was* Life Without Limits *(2007). As a columnist of the* Adventist Review, *he is well known to Adventist readers. He hosts* Cliff! *a regular program on Hope Television. He is the husband of one wife and father of two children.*

References

[1] Wisława Syzmborska, "No Title Required," in *View With a Grain of Sand* (New York: Harcourt, 1995), 175.

[2] William James, *Pragmatism* (Cambridge, Mass.: Hackett Publishing Company, 1981), 118.

[3] C. S. Lewis, *Surprised by Joy* (New York: Harcourt Brace Jovanovich, 1984), 223.

[4] Ibid., 224.

[5] Ibid., 223.

[6] Antony Flew, *There Is a God: How the World's Most Notorious Atheist Changed His Mind* (New York: HarperCollins, 2007).

[7] Ibid., 135.

[8] Ibid., 121.

[9] Bill Bryson, *A Short History of Nearly Everything* (New York: Broadway Books, 2003), 13.

[10] Terrence W. Tilley, "The Problems of Theodicy: A Background Essay," in *Physics and Cosmology,* eds. Nancy Murphy, Robert John Russell, and William R. Stoeger (Vatican City State: Vatican Observatory Publications, 2007), 37.

[11] David Hume, *Dialogues Concerning Natural Religion* (London: Penguin Books, 1990), 53.

[12] Ibid., 56.

[13] Quoted in Flew, *There Is a God,* 131.

[14] Richard Dawkins, *The God Delusion* (New York: Houghton Mifflin Company, 2006), 109.

[15] J. L. Mackie, *The Miracle of Theism* (Oxford: Clarendon, 1982), 116.

[16] Bryan Magee, *Confessions of a Philosopher* (New York: Random House, 1997), 252.

[17] W. H. Auden, "For the Time Being: A Christmas Oratorio," part 3, in *Religious Drama 1*, ed. Marvin Halverson (New York: Meridian, 1957), 17.

[18] J. C. Polkinghorne, *The Faith of a Physicist: Reflections of a Bottom-up Thinker* (Minneapolis: Fortress, 1996), 57.

HUMBERTO M. RASI

Chapter 5

Are Faith and Reason Compatible?

*Lord, help me never to use
my reason against the truth.*

—A Jewish Prayer

Through the centuries, the relationship between faith and reason has been a subject of deep interest for thoughtful Christians. Believers engaged in advanced studies, research, and professions that challenge the foundations of faith are faced with the dilemma of how to integrate faith and reason on a daily basis. This tension is heightened by the fact that many around us assume that intelligent, educated people are not religious or, if they are, believe that such convictions should be kept private.

According to the Scriptures, God created Adam and Eve at the beginning of human history and endowed them with rationality and the power to choose. Exercising those abilities, our first parents disobeyed God and, as a result, lost their perfect condition and their home. Although we have inherited the weaknesses of their fallen condition,

God has preserved our capacity to think for ourselves, exercise trust, and make choices.[1]

Before proceeding, clarity requires that we define three key concepts:

Faith is an act of the will that occurs when one chooses to place ultimate trust in God in response to His self-disclosure and to the promptings of the Holy Spirit in our conscience.[2] Faith is dynamic—it leads to decisions and action. Religious faith is stronger than belief; it includes the willingness to live and even die for one's convictions.

Reason is the exercise of the mental capacity for rational thought, understanding, discernment, and acceptance of a concept or idea. Reason looks for clarity, consistency, coherence, and proper evidence.

Belief is the mental act of accepting as true, factual, or real a statement or a person. Of course, it is also possible to hold a belief in something that is not true.

Reason and faith are asymmetrically related. It is possible to believe that God exists (reason) without believing in God or trusting in Him (faith).[3] But it is impossible to trust in God (faith) without believing that He exists (reason).

While reason is important to faith, it cannot take its place. To a Christian, acquiring knowledge is not life's ultimate goal; life's highest objective is to know God and establish a personal relationship with Him.[4] Such trust and friendship lead to obedience to God and to loving service to fellow human beings.

Relationship between faith and reason

Throughout the Christian era, believers have adopted various approaches to the relationship of faith and reason that can be outlined as follows:[5]

Fideism. *Faith ignores or minimizes the role of reason in arriving at truth.* According to this position, faith in God is the ultimate criterion of truth and is all that a Christian needs for certitude and salvation. Fideists affirm that God reveals Himself to human consciousness through the Scriptures, the Holy Spirit, and mystical experience, which are sufficient to understand all important truths.

Radical fideism extols the value of blind faith in opposition to human reason. Carried to an extreme, fideism rejects rational thought, opposes advanced education and research, and can lead to a private, esoteric religion.

Critics of radical fideism observe that faith in God and in Jesus Christ presupposes a God who has revealed Himself to humanity through Christ. Furthermore, Christians who accept the Bible as a trustworthy revelation of God must necessarily exercise their rational powers to understand Scripture's propositions, exhortations, and prophecies. If the Bible is truly a propositional expression of God's will, as well as the Christian's basis of faith and practice, human reason cannot be disregarded but engaged.

Rationalism. *Human reason challenges, undermines, and eventually destroys religious faith.*

Rationalists maintain that human reason constitutes the foundational source of knowledge and truth, and therefore provides the basis for belief. Modern rationalism rejects supernatural revelation as a source of reliable information.

Beginning with the humanistic revival of the European Renaissance, which extolled human creativity and potential, rationalism flourished during the Enlightenment, with its systematic critique of accepted doctrines and institutions. With time, rationalism developed into different varieties, such as empiricism (Rely on your senses), materialism (Only physical matter and laws can be trusted), pragmatism (Believe in what works), and existentialism (Trust in your personal experience). It eventually evolved into modern skepticism, which questions, doubts, or disagrees with generally accepted conclusions and beliefs and then further still, becoming atheism, where God's existence is denied.

In its opposition to faith, rationalism argues that religions tend to support traditional and sometimes irrational beliefs and frustrate the individual's self-realization. Rationalists also argue that the reality of evil in the world is incompatible with the existence of Christianity's powerful, loving, and wise God.

Dualism. *Faith and reason are autonomous and operate in separate spheres, neither confirming nor contradicting each other.*

This position has been advocated by both agnostic and Christian thinkers. Some maintain that science deals with objective facts, while religion addresses moral issues from a personal, subjective perspective. Therefore, the spheres of activity of reason and faith, knowledge and values, are unrelated to each other.[6]

Bible-believing Christians are not willing to accept this dualism. They argue, for example, that Jesus Christ, as portrayed in the Gospels, is not only the center of their faith as God incarnate, but also a real Person who lived on earth at a particular time and place. They contend that the events narrated and the characters presented in the Scriptures were also real and part of the historical continuum, as shown by a growing volume of documentary and archaeological evidence.

Any attempt to separate the spheres of reason and faith relegates

Christianity to the realm of personal feelings, individual subjectivity, and ultimately to the level of fanciful and irrelevant myth. Both Christians and non-Christians hold to varying and frequently contradictory beliefs. If these cannot be distinguished as to their truthfulness or falsehood by the sole use of reasonable evidence and argument, no belief, whether religious or philosophical, can claim reliability and allegiance.

Synergy. Anchored in God's revelation, reason can strengthen the human quest for and commitment to truth.

Proponents of this position maintain that biblical Christianity constitutes an integrated and internally consistent system of belief and practice that deserves both faith commitment and rational assent.

The realms of faith and reason sometimes overlap. Truths based on faith alone are those revealed by God but not discoverable by human reason (e.g., the Trinity and salvation by God's grace through faith). Truths to which we may arrive through both faith and reason are revealed by God but are also discoverable by human reason (e.g., the existence of God, the objective moral law). Truths ascertained by reason and not by faith are those not directly revealed by God but discovered by the human mind (e.g., mathematical formulas and operations, chemical and physical laws).

If the real world can be comprehended by human reason on the basis of investigation and experience, it is then an intelligible world. The amenability of this world to rational inquiry, both at the cellular and galactic levels, allows humans to discover the laws that provide evidence for intelligent design of the most intricate kind. This extremely elaborate design of all facets of the universe, which makes possible intelligent life on this planet, speaks of a Designer.

Therefore, religious experience and moral conscience[7] can be seen as signs of the existence of the same Being that scientific research envisions as the intelligent Designer of the cosmos and the Sustainer of life.

Reason, then, can help us move from understanding to acceptance and, ideally, to belief. But faith is a choice of the will, a decision to rely on God's revelation as foundational. Careful thinking, under the Holy Spirit's guidance, may remove obstacles on the way to faith; and once faith is already present, reason may strengthen religious commitment.[8]

Faith and reason in biblical perspective

As the early Christian church interacted with the Greco-Roman culture, it began to articulate the distinction between faith and reason, granting to faith the position of privilege in the life of the believer. Bible teaching with respect to faith and reason may be summarized in the following propositions.

The Holy Spirit both awakens faith and illumines reason. If it were not for the persistent influence of the Holy Spirit on human consciousness, no one would ever become a Christian. In our natural condition we do not seek God (Romans 3:10, 11), acknowledge our desperate need of His grace (John 16:7–11), or understand spiritual things (1 Corinthians 2:14). Only through the agency of the Holy Spirit are we drawn to accept, believe, and trust in God (John 16:13, 14). Once this miraculous transformation has occurred (Romans 12:1, 2), the Holy Spirit teaches us (John 14:26), guides us "into all truth" (John 16:13, NIV), and allows us to discern error from falsehood (1 John 4:1–3).

Faith must be exercised and developed during a lifetime. Each human being has been given "a measure of faith" (Romans 12:3, NASB); that is, the capacity to trust in God, and each Christian is encouraged to grow "more and more" in faith (2 Thessalonians 1:3, NIV). In fact, "without faith it is impossible to please God, because anyone who comes to him must believe that he exists and that he rewards those who earnestly seek him" (Hebrews 11:6, NIV). Hence the plea of an anguished father to Jesus: "I do believe; help me overcome my unbelief!" (Mark 9:24, NIV) and the insistent request of the disciples, "Increase our faith!" (Luke 17:5, NIV). We grow in faith when, in response to God's mercy toward us, we increasingly trust Him and follow His commands.

God values and appeals to human reason. Although God's thoughts are infinitely higher than ours (Isaiah 55:8, 9), He has chosen to communicate intelligibly with humankind, revealing Himself through the Scriptures (2 Peter 1:20, 21), through Jesus Christ who called Himself "the truth" (John 14:6, NIV), and in nature, in spite of the effects of the Fall (Psalm 19:1; Genesis 3:14–17; 7:11–24). Jesus frequently engaged His listeners in dialogue and reflection, asking for a thoughtful response (see, e.g., His conversation with Nicodemus, in John 3, and with the Samaritan woman, in John 4). At the request of the Ethiopian official, Philip explained a Messianic prophecy found in Scripture so that he might understand and believe (Acts 8:30–35). The believers in Berea were praised because they "examined the Scriptures every day to see if what Paul said was true" (Acts 17:11, NIV).

God provides enough evidence to believe and trust in Him. The unbiased observer can perceive God's creative and sustaining power in the natural universe (Isaiah 40:26). God's "invisible qualities—his eternal power and divine nature—have been clearly seen" and understood by "what has been made." Those who, in spite of the evidence, insist upon denying His existence and creative power "are without excuse" (Romans 1:20, NIV). Significantly, however, when Thomas expressed doubts about the reality of Christ's resurrection, Christ provided the physical evidence and challenged him to "stop doubting and believe" (John 20:27, NIV). When we are confronted with questions regarding the origin of the universe, our point of departure should be that of faith: "By faith we understand that the universe was formed at God's command, so that what is seen was not made out of what was visible" (Hebrews 11:3, NIV).[9]

Faith and reason can work together in the believer's life and witness. When Jesus was asked to provide a summary of God's law, He stated that the first commandment included, "Love the Lord your God . . . with all your mind" (Mark 12:30, NIV; compare with Deuteronomy 6:4, 5). Paul stated that the acceptance of Christ as Savior depended on a thoughtful understanding of the gospel: "Faith comes from hearing the message, and the message is heard through the word of Christ" (Romans 10:17, NIV). Christians are expected to be "always prepared to give an answer to everyone who asks you to give the reason for the hope that you have" (1 Peter 3:15, NIV).[10] Peter also encourages Christians to "make every effort to add to your faith goodness; and to goodness, knowledge" (2 Peter 1:5, NIV).

Conclusion

It is not difficult to create a gallery of giants of mind and spirit who were Christian believers, such as Paul, Augustine, Luther, Calvin, and Wesley. Modern science emerged in Europe with pioneers of the caliber of Copernicus, Galileo, Kepler, Berkeley, Pascal, Boyle, Newton, Halley, and Linnaeus. All of them had faith in a Creator God who had established in the universe operating laws that could be discovered and applied for the benefit of humanity.

For the educated believer, there is "no incompatibility between vital faith and deep, disciplined, wide-ranging learning, between piety and hard thinking, between the life of faith and the life of the mind."[11]

Like millions of Christians through the ages, I acknowledge the primacy of faith in the intellectual life as expressed in two classical formulations: *Fides quarens intellectum* (Faith seeks understanding) and *Credo ut intelligam* (I believe in order that I may understand).

All of us are called to love God with our entire minds, integrating into our experience the dual demands of faith and intellect. In order to grow both in our trust in God and in our rational abilities, we must deepen each day our friendship with Jesus, our study of the Scriptures, and our commitment to truth.[12]

Humberto M. Rasi *received his college education in his homeland, Argentina, completed a PhD in Hispanic literature and history at Stanford University, and a postdoctoral fellowship at Johns Hopkins University. He served as professor and dean of graduate studies at Andrews University, as editorial vice president at Pacific Press®, and as world director of the Education Department for the Seventh-day Adventist Church (1990–2002). He cofounded the Institute for Christian Teaching, launched the journal* College and University Dialogue, *and has published many articles and edited several books. He and his wife, Julieta, live in Loma Linda, California. They have a son and a daughter involved in their professions, and three granddaughters. Although retired, he continues to lecture, publish, and coordinate projects in international higher education.*

Always Prepared

References

[1] See, e.g., Deuteronomy 29:19, 20; John 6:67–69; Revelation 3:20; 22:17.

[2] Ellen G. White offers a crisp definition: "Faith is trusting God—believing that He loves us and knows best what is for our good." *Education* (Mountain View, Calif.: Pacific Press®, 1952), 253.

[3] "You believe that there is one God. Good! Even the demons believe that—and shudder" (James 2:19). Unless otherwise noted, all Bible passages are quoted from the New International Version.

[4] See Jeremiah 9:23, 24; John 17:3.

[5] See Hugo A. Meynell, "Faith and Reason," in *The Encyclopedia of Modern Christian Thought*, ed. Alister E. McGrath (Oxford: Blackwell, 1993), 214–219.

[6] Stephen Jay Gould (1941–2002), who taught the history of science at Harvard University, stated that "the supposed conflict between science and religion . . . exists only in people's minds and social practices, not in the logic or proper utility of these entirely different, and equally vital subjects." In his view, "Science tries to document the factual character of the natural world, and to develop theories that coordinate and explain these facts. Religion, on the other hand, operates in the equally important, but utterly different, realm of human purposes, meanings, and values." *Rock of Ages: Science and Religion in the Fullness of Life* (New York: Ballentine, 1999), 3, 4.

[7] The apostle Paul argues thus, "(Indeed, when Gentiles, who do not have the law, do by nature things required by the law, they are a law for themselves, even though they do not have the law, since they show that the requirements of the law are written on their hearts, their consciences also bearing witness, and their thoughts now accusing, now even defending them)" (Romans 2:14, 15).

[8] See Richard Rice, *Reason and the Contours of Faith* (Riverside, Calif.: La Sierra University Press, 1991).

[9] Ellen G. White states, "God never asks us to believe, without giving sufficient evidence upon which to base our faith. His existence, His character, the truthfulness of His world, are all established by testimony that appeals to our reason; and this testimony is abundant. Yet God has never removed the possibility of doubt. Our faith must rest upon evidence, not demonstration. Those who wish to doubt will have opportunity; while those who really desire to know the truth will find plenty of evidence on which to rest their faith." *Steps to Christ* (Mountain View, Calif.: Pacific Press®, 1892), 105.

[10] The original Greek of this passage includes two significant words: *apología*, "answer, defense, justification"; *logos*, "reason, word, explanation."

[11] Arthur F. Holmes, *Building the Christian Academy* (Grand Rapids, Mich.: Eerdmans, 2001), 5.

[12] Readers interested in a longer version of this essay, titled "Faith, Reason, and Choice: Loving God With All Our Mind," may access the text at http://fae.adventist.org/essays/31Bcc_337-354.htm.

WILLIAM G. JOHNSSON

Chapter 6

What's Unique About Jesus?

I find it impossible to tell you why I think Jesus is unique in a dispassionate, depersonalized manner. To write about Him is to open up my own life: His story became my story. Jesus of Nazareth has profoundly impacted the course of my life—and, I am absolutely confident—for the better.

Once when Jesus was with His disciples, He asked them, "Who do people say the Son of Man is?" They gave various answers that were floating around—John the Baptist, Elijah, Jeremiah, and so on. Then He fixed them with His eyes and asked, "Who do you say I am?" (Matthew 16:13–20, NIV).

That is still the really *big* question. It is more important than anything we will have to answer in a tough examination because the way we deal with it will shape our lives. Whatever responses we give, we will not be the same forever after.

I urge you: Work your own way through to the answer. Don't trust anyone else's opinions or views. It's got to be *your* answer.

How to start? Start where I did—read and reread the story of Jesus. The New Testament has four accounts, all different and in places surprisingly different, but in a strange way coming together to give a unified portrait of a remarkable Person.

You can trust these accounts. They are very early, three written within thirty years of Jesus' death, and the other one—the Gospel of John—following maybe thirty years later. They are all based on eyewitness accounts; they ring true.

Now, a lot of people today, including some scholars, will tell you that you can't rely on these accounts. They argue that we really cannot know what Jesus was like or what He actually said and that the idea that He was anything more than a mere man was something that came much later, an invention of His followers. Sometimes the arguments seem convincing, but study them carefully and you will find them full of holes. For instance, some scholars give equal weight to the so-called Gospel of Judas, written in the mid- to late-second century, with the eyewitness accounts that constitute the four biblical Gospels. This is arrant nonsense.[1]

So read the Gospels—Matthew, Mark, Luke, John. As you read, think about this Man who dominates every page. Try reading each Gospel at one sitting, skipping chapter breaks (they were added later). And see what sort of figure emerges in your head. See if you don't find Jesus to be like I found Him—absolutely unique.

On one level, Jesus is so ordinary—a poor person, uneducated, a carpenter who becomes an itinerant teacher-healer. There were plenty of others like that in the Palestine of His time.

And yet, and yet—almost everything about Jesus is so *extraordinary*. He is different; He amazes by what He does and what He doesn't do; by what He teaches and what He doesn't teach. He is unique. In at least seven ways He is unique: in impact, in birth, in life, in teachings, in what He claims about Himself, in death, and in continuing presence.

Unique in impact

Whatever interpretation you give to the Gospel accounts, you can't escape one fact: Jesus of Nazareth was a dynamic Figure who created waves everywhere He went. Meek and mild He was not, the beloved children's song to the contrary.

He goes to the synagogue on Sabbath in Capernaum and conducts an exorcism. Everyone is shocked: "Who is this?" they question. He returns to His hometown of Nazareth, and they want Him to put on a show for the good old boys. They ask Him to speak and He infuriates them by showing from the Scriptures that they can claim no special privilege with God. At last, they throw Him out and try to lynch Him.

He visits Jerusalem and goes to the temple. Seeing the desecration of the house of prayer by all the buying and selling, He lashes the merchants, drives out the sheep and cattle, and turns the money changers' tables upside down. They flee in panic from this angry Man.

Quite soon the religious establishment realizes the threat He poses to their authority. The leaders begin to plot to kill Him. The schemes take time to work out, but at last they have their way: Jesus of Nazareth hangs on a Roman cross. It's a bloody, excruciating form of execution—the worst way to die.

No weakling, this Man. No gentle Jesus, meek and mild.

They kill Him, but they can't kill His impact. His little band of followers, who abandoned Him when He was arrested, become convinced that He has conquered death. They go everywhere—north and south, east and west—with the good news that in Jesus of Nazareth God has provided life, new life, life to the full right now, and life unending after this existence.

The good news rolls on and on. In the face of threats, torture, lashings, jail, the fiery stake, the Colosseum, it is unstoppable. Jesus of Nazareth brings the gods of Rome and Greece to their knees.

It has never stopped. It has won the world. And everywhere it has gone the love and compassion of its Lord have brought hospitals and hospices, healing and hope. True, there is another side of history: Jesus has not always been represented well by those who take His name, nor is He represented well today. But on balance, His impact has been overwhelmingly positive.

Jesus is the most influential Person who ever lived. We count years by reference to His coming to earth. As biblical scholar Reynolds Price asserts, "It would require much exotic calculation, however, to deny that the single most powerful figure—not merely in these two millenniums but in all of human history—has been Jesus of Nazareth. . . . A serious argument can be made that no one else's life has proved as remotely as powerful and enduring as that of Jesus."[2]

His is the most unlikely "success story" imaginable. An uneducated Carpenter who dies young, executed, but who captures the hearts and minds of more people in history—what Hollywood writer would try to sell that script?

Unique in birth

Whenever Jesus referred to His father, it was always the Father in heaven. Not once did He speak of Joseph, the husband of Mary, as His father.

Two of the Gospels, Matthew and Luke, recount the story of Jesus' birth, and both assert that Mary, a virgin, was pregnant with Jesus when she married Joseph. Both accounts attribute her pregnancy to the intervention of the Holy Spirit.

Questions concerning the circumstances of Jesus' birth led to sneers from those who opposed His ministry. "We were not born of fornication," they taunted—implying that He was. Jesus, however, apparently never felt the need to respond directly. Throughout His ministry He consistently spoke about having come "from heaven" to this earth, and of returning to heaven after His work was done.[3]

The virgin birth of Jesus, if true, makes Him utterly unique among the billions of people who have ever lived. Critics, understandably, have attacked the idea, just as they did in His own time. But the larger issue concerns what one makes of miracles. If, as many today hold, the universe is a closed system operating by unchanging natural processes, miracles must have to be ruled out of court.

But if God exists, the equation changes dramatically. Now the supernatural intersects with the natural, and a setting aside of the usual can be entertained. That means miracles.

If, as the Scriptures clearly teach and I believe, Jesus' birth involved the intervention of the divine in the human, He is the God-man. He is truly God, and truly human.

Unique in life

What makes a life unique? Some historians look to military conquests, as with Alexander, who is termed "the Great." But was Alexander greater than Aristotle? Or Mozart than Mother Teresa? How about Einstein and Schweitzer?

Jesus has never been called "Jesus the Great." We recoil from such a designation. It doesn't fit Him; His life is unique. Such a life! Such simplicity, such nobility! Such clearness of purpose, such humility! Such agreement between words and practice! Such purity, such selflessness!

As I contemplate the life of Jesus as portrayed by the Gospel writers, several characteristics jump out: never too busy to stop and help, love of children, one-on-one conversations, thoughtfulness, unceasing outpouring of love and compassion, and Friend of the marginalized. Jesus lives a full life, but He finds time to talk with the Samaritan woman who comes to the well to draw water. When parents bring their little ones, He takes them in His arms and pronounces terrible judgment on anyone who would hurt them. He reaches out to touch the leper. And even with His dying breath, He makes provision for His mother's care.

What a life! Never another like His. Well has it been said that if God should take human form, it would be like Jesus of Nazareth. And God did!

Unique in teachings

In content and mode, Jesus' teachings resemble in some respects those of Jewish rabbis before Him and the great thinkers of the world. In the one aspect that forms their heart, however, His teachings are unique.

Grace—there is nothing like it in all the wisdom of the world. The religions of mankind address issues of life and death, of pain and suffering. They all point the way to break free of the shackles of mortality by showing what we have to do to please God, escape annihilation, and so on.

Then Jesus comes on the scene. God is on your side, He proclaims. God is your heavenly Father, watching over you now and eager to have you live with Him forever. With hypocrites and all who play religious games, He is severe, but all who seek find in Him peace, joy, rest. Heaven opens, not to the strong and the brave, but to those who simply accept it as a gift freely given by a loving God.

This is grace: Heaven's best for the unworthy, for the broken, for the nobodies. Instead of the challenge: "Come to Me, you who are rich, learned, worthy," the invitation goes out: "Come to Me, you who are poor and unworthy." Jesus said, "Blessed are the poor in spirit, for theirs is the kingdom of heaven" (Matthew 5:3, NIV).

And that is how Jesus lived. He taught grace, and He lived it.

Unique in claims

Jesus said outrageous things about Himself. When Peter, responding to His question, "Who do you say that I am?" declared, "You are the Christ [Messiah], the Son of the living God," Jesus did not deny the words. Rather, He remarked that Peter's insight came from Heaven itself. Again, when He stood before the kangaroo court and the high priest demanded, "[Tell us,] are you . . . the Son of the Blessed One?" He replied, "I am."[4]

Jesus regarded Himself as altogether other. God was His Father, and no one could come to the Father except through Him. "I am the way, the truth, and the life"; "I am the light of the world"; "I am the bread of life"; "I am the good shepherd"; "I am the resurrection and the life"; "I am the true vine"—statements like these were the height of religious arrogance— unless they were true. And capping them all, this: "I and the Father are one"; "Before Abraham was born, I am," thus identifying Himself with eternal, self-existent deity.[5]

And Jesus acted on these claims. He declared sins forgiven; He reinterpreted Sabbath observance, because, He said, He was the Lord of the Sabbath; He healed the sick, working as His father worked before Him.

We cannot pass by these claims lightly. We lock up people who talk like this; or else we have to face the possibility that Jesus really was what He said.[6]

Unique in death

Jesus was crucified—nothing unique in that. Thousands of others over the centuries were executed in the same way by Rome. But what came after He died that Friday afternoon was totally different from all the other deaths on crosses.

A separate essay in this book gives extended treatment to Jesus' death and resurrection, so I will simply note here two salient points: the empty tomb and the rise of the Christian church. Something happened to Jesus' body—it disappeared. And out of the ashes of that bleak Friday's execution, a new movement sprang up, proclaiming that Jesus had conquered death.

Unique in continuing presence

For those who believe in Jesus, this is the climactic fact that makes Him unique. Other great men and women are dead and gone, but in a mysterious manner Jesus is not. He is alive! We cannot see Him, but we can know Him—know Him as Someone as real as a friend. We can know him, love Him, adore Him as Savior and Lord.

Ancient words from the first Christians leap across the centuries, echo the cry of our hearts today: "Though you have not seen him, you love him; and even though you do not see him now, you believe in him and are filled with an inexpressible and glorious joy."[7]

Because of this fact—His continuing presence—Christianity has not died out, will never die away. This is why the story of Jesus goes on and on, ever new to each generation, ever fresh, offering better life, life more abundant.

So what's unique about Jesus? Almost everything! Let Philip Yancey have the final word: "*Why am I a Christian?* I sometimes ask myself, and to be perfectly honest the reasons reduce to two: (1) The lack of good alternatives, and (2) Jesus. Brilliant, untamed, tender, creative, slippery, irreducible, paradoxically humble—Jesus stands up to scrutiny. He is who I want my God to be."[8]

For further reading:

Ball, Bryan W., and William G. Johnsson, eds. *The Essential Jesus*. Boise, Idaho: Pacific Press®, 2002.

Lewis, C. S. *Mere Christianity*. Various editions available, from 1952 onwards.

Strobel, Lee. *The Case for Christ*. Grand Rapids, Mich.: Zondervan, 1998.

———. *The Case for Faith*. Grand Rapids, Mich.: Zondervan, 1998.

Zacharias, Ravi. *Jesus Among Other Gods*. Nashville, Tenn.: Word, 2000.

Always Prepared

William G. Johnsson *is assistant to the president for Interfaith Relations at the General Conference. And this is in his retirement! Fifteen years of teaching in India were followed by five at the Adventist Theological Seminary, Andrews University. From 1982 until 2006, he was editor of the* Adventist Review. *Under his tutelage* Adventist World *came into being in 2005. His degrees come from three continents: two bachelor's degrees from Australia, his home country; a BD from London University; a PhD in biblical studies from Vanderbilt University in 1973, and a DDiv (honoris causa) from Andrews in 2007. He is the author of twenty-two books and thousands of published articles. His hobbies include long-distance running, gardening, and his and Noelene's grandchildren.*

References

[1] See F. F. Bruce, *The New Testament Documents: Are They Reliable?* (Grand Rapids, Mich.: Eerdmans, 2003).

[2] Reynolds Price, "Jesus of Nazareth Then and Now," *Time,* December 6, 1999.

[3] John 8:41, NASB; John 3:13, NASB.

[4] Matthew 16:13–20, NIV; Mark 14:61, 62, NIV.

[5] John 14:6; 8:12; 6:35; 10:14; 11:25; 15:1; 10:30; 8:58, NIV.

[6] Note C. S. Lewis's challenge: "Either this man was, and is, the Son of God: or else a madman or something worse. You can shut Him up for a fool, you can spit at Him and kill Him as a demon; or you can fall at His feet and call Him Lord and God. But let us not come with any patronizing nonsense about His being a great human teacher. He has not left that open to us." *Mere Christianity* (New York: Collier-Macmillan, n.d.), 56.

[7] 1 Peter 1:8, NIV.

[8] Philip Yancey, *The Jesus I Never Knew* (Grand Rapids, Mich.: Zondervan, 1995), 265; emphasis in original.

DAVID MARSHALL

Chapter 7

Did Jesus Really Come Back to Life?

The Christian church is built on belief in the bodily resurrection of Jesus.

The birth and rapid rise of the Christian church remains an unsolved enigma for anyone who refuses to accept the one explanation offered by the church itself: the bodily resurrection of Jesus. Disprove it and you have disposed of Christianity.

Few have expressed this thought as well as Pulitzer Prize-winner John Updike (1932–2009). Associated in the public mind with stylish novels, Updike encountered Christianity in the writings of Søren Kierkegaard and Karl Barth and continued to be a believing Christian for the rest of his life. These lines are from Updike's "Seven Stanzas at Easter":

> Make no mistake: if He rose at all
> it was as His body;
> if the cells' dissolution did not reverse, the molecules
> reknit, the amino acids rekindle,

> the Church will fall. . . .
>
> Let us not mock God with metaphor,
> analogy, sidestepping, transcendence;
> making of the event a parable, a sign painted in the
> faded credulity of earlier ages:
> let us walk through the door.
>
> The stone is rolled back, not papier-mâché,
> not a stone in a story,
> but the vast rock of materiality that in the slow
> grinding of time will eclipse for each of us
> the wide light of day.[1]

To counter the apostles' assertion that Jesus rose bodily from the tomb, the scientific rationalist responds, "Well then, let's watch what happens when people die." And he or she demonstrates that those who die are buried, decay, and, ultimately, merge with the ground around them. His or her argument is that Jesus' resurrection could not have happened because it is not repeatable.

However, miracles are, by definition, unprecedented events. Hence it is not logically valid to use science as an argument against them. Science—based on the observation of precedents—can have nothing to say about the bodily resurrection of Jesus. Philosophical speculation is similarly inappropriate. We do not have an infallible knowledge of natural law, so we cannot exclude from the outset every possibility of unique events.

The case against a miracle is only acceptable when every report of that miracle has been investigated and found to be false. Such investigation is the work of a historian. And the historian cannot adjudicate upon what history may or may not contain. His job is to investigate the primary sources objectively and to report accordingly. The historicity of the bodily resurrection of Jesus should be determined by the examination of the testimonies of witnesses and the reliability of the available primary sources.

We must examine (1) the nature of the sources, (2) the evidence for the death of Jesus, and (3) the evidence for the bodily resurrection of Jesus.

The sources

Among the earliest sources on the Resurrection, Paul's first letter to the Corinthian Christians was written in A.D. 54.[2] The importance of 1 Corinthians 15 as a primary source is hard to exaggerate, especially since, in its first half-dozen verses, Paul is quoting a much earlier source that had its origins among the apostles in the earliest post-Pentecost period.[3]

Paul (originally Saul of Tarsus) had been the most hostile opponent of Christianity before his own encounter with the risen Christ. The post-Pentecost fragment with which he begins chapter 15 is the generally accepted statement of Resurrection eyewitnesses. Peter and James—the James who became the leader of the Jerusalem church—are listed first. Then come the risen Lord's appearances to the disciple groups and His appearance "to more than five hundred of the brothers at the same time" to which Paul added the editorial point, "most of whom are still living, though some have fallen asleep" (1 Corinthians 15:5, 6, NIV). The implication of that point is clear: If you aren't convinced, go and talk to them.

The historical importance of such a statement is huge. It was made in what the most authoritative scholars authenticate as a genuine letter written by someone in close touch with other eyewitnesses, less than twenty-five years after an event that happened nearly two thousand years ago. Few, if any, ancient events are supported by such early and sound evidence.

Three of the narrative accounts of the Resurrection (Matthew 28; Mark 16; Luke 24) were written from eyewitness accounts in the years between the first letter to the Corinthians and the fall of Jerusalem (A.D. 54–70). The fourth narrative account (John 20) was an eyewitness account, too, but written in Ephesus towards the end of the first century.

Among the four accounts, there are variations in detail inevitable in eyewitness reports. These suggest that there had been no collusion. John Wenham reconciles the variations by explaining that each account was from a different perspective and arguing that none of the reporters was attempting to tell the whole story. John was writing from a deeply personal perspective.[4] In his letter to Corinth, Paul had marshaled his evidence in a quasi-judicial fashion and, aware that a woman's testimony was not valid in a law court, had simply excluded the witness of the women. The authors of the four narrative accounts gave themselves no such constraints. The earliest witnesses on the day in question had been women. Considerations of legal plausibility (given the status of women in first-century Palestine) were insufficient to alter the facts and, therefore, insufficient to warrant the exclusion of the female witnesses.

Each account is unequivocally clear that the resurrection of Jesus was a verified and witnessed historical event. As Paul said before King Agrippa, the death and resurrection of Jesus had not been "done in a corner" (Acts 26:26, NIV). There were plenty of contemporaries of Jesus and participants in the events who were still around and could have challenged the accounts in circulation (those of Paul, Mark, Matthew, and Luke, in particular). None would appear to have done so.

Evidence for the death of Jesus

Prior to crucifixion, Jesus had been whipped viciously. Jewish rules limited the number of lashes to thirty-nine, but it is unlikely that the Romans were bound by that limitation. The *flagrum* used for the whipping had long leather thongs of varying lengths, each with sharp jagged pieces of bone and lead attached to them. In the course of thirty-nine lashes across the back and legs of the prisoner, the blows would cut through the subcutaneous tissue, rendering the back an unrecognizable mass of torn, bleeding tissue. Many did not survive the thirty-nine lashes.[5]

Israeli archaeologists have learned a lot about crucifixion from recent excavations on Mount Scopus. A seven-inch spike was driven through both heel bones. A heavy wrought-iron spike was driven through the front of the wrist, causing the incomplete severing of the median nerve. Because of the person's position, air would be drawn into the lungs, which could not be exhaled. Carbon dioxide would build up in the lungs and the bloodstream. Death came by suffocation.[6]

When Jesus was reported dead at 3 P.M. on Good Friday, "One of the soldiers pierced Jesus' side with a spear, *bringing a sudden flow of blood and water*" (John 19:34, NIV; emphasis added). The witness who saw this and later wrote it down did not understand its significance. "Nobody did until the rise of modern medicine. . . . This is evidence of massive clotting of blood in the main arteries, and is exceptionally strong medical proof of death. . . . The 'blood and water' is proof positive that Jesus was dead."[7]

Romans had not been the first to inflict crucifixion, but they made the most use of it and were most grimly efficient in its practice. There were no survivors.

Evidence for the bodily resurrection

Two senior members of the Jewish ruling council, who had a sense of injustice with regard to the brutal way in which Jesus had been judicially murdered, sought and received permission from the Roman governor to remove the body from the cross. They prepared it for burial and interred it in a rock-hewn tomb that one of them, Joseph of Arimathea, had commissioned for his own use.[8]

A stone, which a modern authority has estimated as between one-and-a-half and two tons in weight, was rolled over the tomb entrance. A Roman seal was placed on it and, at the request of the leaders of the Jewish ruling council hostile to Jesus, the Roman authorities posted an armed guard next to the tomb. Most authorities accept that it was a sixteen-man Roman security detachment. Flavius Fegitius Renatus was typical of Roman military historians of that period in insisting that discipline in the Roman legions was stricter during the reign of Tiberius than at any subsequent time.[9]

The ancient world knew that resurrection did not and could not happen. Following the Crucifixion, the disciples of Jesus were broken, angry, and disillusioned. They experienced a horrific "crisis of faith."[10]

Had first-century people set out to invent a story about resurrection, they would not have given the starring role to a woman—let alone Mary Magdalene. With other women, she approached the tomb, weeping. Finding the tomb empty, they wept more. The loss of the body was the final indignity in a trauma that had begun with the arrest late at night on Thursday. To discover the absence of the body was to feel that even their grief had been violated. The discovery of the empty tomb—and subsequent encounter with the risen Christ—by women was apt to make the story unbelievable to contemporary Jews. When told the story, the male disciples "did not believe the women, because their words seemed to them like nonsense" (Luke 24:11, NIV).

Nevertheless, something approaching hope must have dawned in the minds of Peter and John. Both ran to the empty tomb at their different paces, John arriving first but hesitating to enter, and Peter bringing up the rear but blundering on into the tomb. John was convinced that resurrection had taken place when he saw the grave clothes. Peter and the others believed as, over a period of days, they encountered the risen Lord.

Accounts agree, however, that Mary Magdalene had seen Him first and had recognized Him when He used her name. Jesus appeared in a variety of locations, mostly to groups of sizes varying between two and five hundred, and did so over a period of forty days (Acts 1:3). What they saw and experienced made Pentecost heroes of the Gethsemane cowards. And their heroism was not short lived. The disciple who had denied knowing Jesus on the night of His arrest when a servant girl confronted him, was the one who, before the ruling council some weeks later, was both strong and defiant (Acts 4:8–12). His transformation was typical of the others.

From Pentecost on—with the empty tomb as exhibit A—thousands of Jews, including priests, accepted the truth of the Resurrection from the vocal and valorous disciples. From Easter Sunday on, all the efforts of the Jewish authorities were meant to suppress reports of what had happened. The disciples preached that God had raised Jesus from the dead in vindication of His divinity and in acceptance of His sacrifice for sinners. So what did the Jewish authorities think had happened? What were they trying to suppress? Why bribe the soldiers and, subsequently, screen them from punishment?

The tomb was empty. No one could say otherwise, so no one did. If the authorities believed the story they had bribed the soldiers to tell—that the disciples had stolen the body while they slept (Matthew 28:11–15)—why was no attempt made to find and produce the body?

It is clear that the soldiers, the Jewish leaders and, perhaps, the governor himself *knew* that something supernatural had happened and that they engaged in a futile attempt to keep the lid on the story.[11] That is among the reasons why Pinchas Lapide, an orthodox Jewish rabbi, in *The Resurrection of Jesus,* reached the conclusion: "I accept the resurrection of Jesus not as an invention of the community of disciples, but as a historical event."[12] The evidence warrants that conclusion.

Belief in the Resurrection did not arise because the disciples were expecting one. Far from it. Further, an objective encounter of the disciples with the risen Jesus is the only way we can explain their subsequent behavior and, as a result, the growth of the church. Visions and subjective experiences would not have done it. These men were imprisoned, tortured, and killed in all manner of grisly ways. They would not have done that in defense of a lie. "I have seen the Lord!" they exclaimed. The Lord had shown them His hands and His side. He had *spoken* and *walked* with them, had *distributed food* to them and *eaten* with them, had *performed signs, given a blessing with His hands,* and *been touched.*[13]

The Jewish leaders showed their political skill in handling the Roman governor. It would have required little skill on their part to have handled Christ's followers had they known the location of the body. Instead, they were reduced to hauling the disciples in from time to time in order to threaten them with what they would do if they did not stop preaching the risen Christ (Acts 5:17–42).

The swoon theory—that Jesus survived flagellation followed by crucifixion and a spear in His side, somehow regained consciousness in the tomb, extricated Himself from the grave clothes, pushed away the stone, and walked miles on pierced feet to be hailed as the Conqueror of death—has never been given credence by scholars.

How could such a Savior have changed the sorrow of the disciples into joy, defeat into victory and fired up "the winged thunderbolt" that was the early church? If such a fraud was at the foundation of Christianity, why did so many Christians submit to be beaten, imprisoned, tortured, and executed? Under pressure of death would not some of them, at least, break and recant?

Richard Swinburne, who has examined the case for the Resurrection from the scientific-rationalist position, reaches the conclusion that "the detailed historical evidence [is] so strong [that,] despite the fact that such a resurrection would be a violation of natural laws, . . . the balance of probability [is] . . . in favour of the resurrection."[14]

A dispassionate lawyer or historian might consider the case proven.

Easter faith did not manufacture the facts. On the contrary, "the events of Easter gave rise to this astonishing and world-changing faith."[15]

For further reading:

Ball, Bryan W., and William G. Johnsson, eds. *The Essential Jesus*. Boise, Idaho: Pacific Press®, 2002.

Beasley-Murray, P. *The Message of the Resurrection*. Leicester, UK: InterVarsity Press, 2000.

Davis, S., D. Kendall, and G. O'Collins, eds. *The Resurrection: An Interdisciplinary Symposium on the Resurrection of Jesus*. Oxford: Oxford University Press, 1997.

Green, Michael. *The Message of Matthew*. Leicester, UK: InterVarsity Press, 2000.

Milne, Bruce. *The Message of John*. Leicester, UK: InterVarsity Press, 1993.

Morris, Leon. *The Gospel According to St. Luke*. Rev. ed. Tyndale New Testament Commentaries. Leicester, UK: InterVarsity Press, 1988.

Strobel, Lee. *The Case for Christ*. Grand Rapids, Mich.: Zondervan, 1998.

Wenham, J. *The Easter Enigma: Are the Resurrection Accounts in Conflict?* Carlisle, UK: Paternoster Press, 1996.

Wright, N. T., and M. Borg. *The Meaning of Jesus*. London: SPCK, 1999.

David Marshall received his undergraduate and postgraduate education at the University of Hull, England. He did his PhD research under one of Britain's most eminent historians, Professor J. P. Kenyon. The skills used in his analysis of the evidences for the Resurrection here and elsewhere are those of the professional historian. He has been senior editor of the Stanborough Press, the Adventist publishing house serving Europe and Africa. He has published thirty books, lives with his wife, Anita, in Grantham, England, and is part of a large four-generation family residing in England and Wales, all of whom are Seventh-day Adventists.

References

[1] John Updike, "Seven Stanzas at Easter," in *Telephone Poles, and Other Poems* (New York: Knopf, 1963), quoted in Bruce Milne, *The Message of John* (Leicester, UK: InterVarsity Press, 1993), 293, 294.

[2] David Prior, *The Message of 1 Corinthians* (Leicester, UK: InterVarsity Press, 2000), 14.

[3] Michael Green, *The Empty Cross of Jesus* (London: Hodder and Stoughton, 1984), 96, 97.

[4] John Wenham, *The Easter Enigma: Are the Resurrection Accounts in Conflict?* (Exeter, UK: Paternoster, 1996).

[5] C. T. Davis, "The Crucifixion of Jesus," *Arizona Medicine*, March 1965, 185.

[6] J. McDowell, *The Resurrection Factor* (Amersham, UK: Scripture Press, 1988), 61–65.

[7] Green, *The Empty Cross of Christ*, 92, 93.

[8] On the burial of Jesus (John 19 and 20), see Milne, *The Message of John*, 285–292; C. G. Kruse, *John*, Tyndale New Testament Commentaries (Leicester, UK: InterVarsity Press, 2003), 369–374.

[9] See David N. Marshall, "The Risen Jesus," in *The Essential Jesus: The Man, His Message, His Mission*, eds. B. W. Ball and W. G. Johnsson (Boise, Idaho: Pacific Press®, 2002), 180–191.

[10] G. O'Collins, *Contemporary Christian Insights: Interpreting Jesus* (London: Mowbray, 1983), 115; Green, *The Empty Cross of Christ*, 102.

[11] Wenham, *The Easter Enigma*, 78–80.

[12] Pinchas Lapide, *The Resurrection of Jesus*, quoted in Green, *The Empty Cross of Christ*, 103.

[13] Matthew 28:1, 7, 9, 18–20; Luke 24:13–16, 30, 34, 39–46, 50; John 20:14, 18, 20, 30; Acts 1:3, 4; 1 Corinthians 15:5–8.

[14] R. Swinburne, "Evidence for the Resurrection," in *The Resurrection: An Interdisciplinary Symposium on the Resurrection of Jesus*, eds. S. David, D. Kendall and G. O'Collins (Oxford: Oxford University Press, 1997), 202.

[15] Green, *The Empty Cross of Christ*, 119.

Chapter 8

How Can Miracles Be Possible?

The subject of miracles is tantalizing. On the one hand, it impinges upon some of the core issues of the Christian faith and yet it scandalizes the modern mind. The word *miracle* is from the Latin *miraculum,* which means "wonder." Therefore, evangelical theologian Wayne Grudem is correct in defining a miracle as a "less common kind of God's activity in which he arouses people's awe and wonder and bears witness to himself."[1] But the Bible does not have a single word for the concept because, besides the idea of wonder (the primary notion), a miracle in the Bible suggests a mighty work (1 Kings 17:17–24; Luke 7:11–17) as well as a sign (Exodus 4:1–9; John 10:38). Of course, it is helpful to know these shades of meaning in the biblical concept of a miracle, but in order to answer the question how miracles can be possible, more needs to be said about the nature of miracles. We ask the question about the possibility of miracles because these are a group of phenomena whose reality is often in doubt. But, to what class of reality do miracles belong? Or do they? These questions must be clearly addressed first before determining if miracles are possible and under what conditions they may be possible. In our defense of the possibility of miracles, we will endeavor to show that the bases on which they are denied are shaky, and that belief in theism removes most obstacles.

Christians on the nature of miracles

Christians reserve the term *miracle* for a particular class of God's activities. Theologians usually categorize God's acts into *creation* (the initial act of bringing the universe into being) and *providence* (His ongoing preservation of the creation). They go on further to distinguish the customary way in which God acts to preserve the creation from His special providential acts. The former are His *providentia ordinaria* (ordinary providence) and the latter, His *providentia extraordinaria* (extraordinary providence).[2] Miracles are usually identified with the latter category. However, some will keep miracles out of the extraordinary category, restricting the latter to those events in which God appears to order natural causes to bring about His purposes (such as God causing an earthquake to secure the release of Paul and Silas from prison [Acts 16:25, 26]).[3] It is possible to include miracles in the category of extraordinary providence, but taking them out of that category emphasizes their lack of connection with any natural causes. In view of how modernity has related to miracles, taking this approach could be helpful in answering the question posed by this chapter.

Modernity on the nature of miracles

Since the rise of science and historical criticism during the age of the Enlightenment, the credibility of miracles has been attacked, based on the customary modern definition of a miracle as "a violation of a law of nature."[4] On this account miracles are deemed contradictory (Voltaire, 1694–1778) or improbable (David Hume, 1711–1776). On the one hand, even if we assume that the modern definition is right, it does not follow logically that miracles do not occur. On the other hand, the modern definition could be defective. When the concept of a violation of natural law is analyzed from the perspective of all three contemporary views or theories of natural law, it is shown to be intrinsically incoherent and flawed. The three theories are (1) the regularity theory, (2) the nomic necessity theory, and (3) the causal disposition theory.[5]

The *regularity theory* of natural law says that the so-called laws of nature are not laws at all. They are just a description of the regularities we observe in nature. Therefore, on this view, a natural law should properly be a generalized account of whatever happens in nature. If this is the case, how can a miraculous event happening in the realm of nature be said to violate natural law?

The *nomic necessity theory* of natural law is not very different from the regularity theory. It simply goes beyond the merely descriptive "regularity theory," to say that natural laws are what enable us to make judgments about what can or cannot happen in the natural world. In other words, based on experience, the nomic necessity theory facilitates universal generalization of an inductive sort about nature. Here again, it does not make sense to say, in the event of a miraculous event, that natural law has been violated. Consistency would require that when a "miracle" happens the existing universal generalization ought to be modified to accommodate the new phenomenon.

The *causal disposition theory* of natural law begins with the assumption that things have certain innate powers (propensities) that, unimpeded, will lead to certain results in nature. Natural laws, therefore, are the necessary truths about these causal dispositions in things. If something is not naturally disposed to cause some things to happen, they cannot happen. A miracle under this theory would be an interruption of the propensities a thing possesses. But why should such an interruption, if it should occur, be labeled a violation of the laws of nature? If, for example, through God's interruption in a certain situation salt failed to dissolve in water, that would not mean that salt as a substance no longer has the natural propensity to dissolve in water! What it would mean is that it is possible for salt to continue to have the disposition to dissolve in water and still be made, in a miraculous situation, to not dissolve.

The truth seems to be that contemporary natural law theories overreach in stating the case of what is possible in nature. Human beings set rules regarding what can happen in nature. And when things happen outside of the rules, they describe them as violations of the "laws of nature," and therefore inadmissible. Ideally, when things happen that seem to be scientific anomalies, natural laws should be revised to accommodate them. Unfortunately, natural laws are rigidly conceived with a built-in "all things being equal" assumption. Therefore, so-called scientific anomalies are not allowed to challenge the basic premise of natural causation built into natural laws. Since in all situations it is assumed that some natural factors must be causing the anomaly, natural law theories are not allowed to be violated and revised. There is no logical reason why, in a so-called scientific anomaly, one may not assume that some supernatural factors may be at work. But as it is, natural law theories have been construed to be valid only on the assumption that no supernatural factor can be at play. It is this arbitrary naturalistic requirement that appears to give one the credibility of talking about violations of the laws of nature. Once this condition is dropped, it will make no more sense to talk about violations of natural laws. Nature's dispositions or propensities may be more "accommodating" or broader than the rules human beings set for them. What those inclined to modern thinking should be saying is *not* that miracles are violations of the laws of nature, rather that miracles are events that, given certain natural conditions at a time and place, cannot be produced by the relevant natural causes. The real question, then, is whether the very natural impossibility of a genuine miracle should force the conclusion that no event may be identified as a miracle. David Hume thought so.

Physical impossibility does not deny the reality of miracles

Hume is recognized as the most significant and influential voice in Western philosophy to provide a definition of miracles that denies the possibility of their happening in the ordinary course of nature. In his *An Enquiry Concerning Human Understanding,* Hume observes, "A miracle may be accurately defined, a transgression of a law of nature by a particular volition of the deity, or by the interposition of some invisible agent."[6] The definition is part of the conclusion to his argument that one "may establish it as a maxim that, no human testimony can have such a force as to prove a miracle, and make it a just foundation for any such system of religion."[7] Thus, although it seems that Hume's definition could make room for miracles, in reality, his point was to deny them. His premise was always that it was more rational to believe that some mistake or deception was afoot than to believe in the genuine occurrence of a miracle.[8] Following Hume's lead, it has become commonplace to believe that the occurrence of a genuine miracle is by definition naturally impossible.

In view of the foregoing skepticism, how may we defend the reality of miracles? First, it should be noted again that the fact that miracles may be naturally impossible does not mean that they do not occur. Natural or physical impossibility does not mean logical impossibility. The argument that miracles are impossible because they transgress natural laws fails to give a complete account of the nature of law. George Mavrodes argues persuasively that in spite of the arguments suggesting that laws of nature are different from legal laws or codes, both display structural parallelisms: the term *law* is used for both, and they both intend to indicate universal generalizations.[9] Logically, if the law that requires all taxpayers to file their returns before April 15 remains the law (a universal generalization) in spite of some actual violations of it, it is illogical to deny actual miracles because some so-called humanly constructed law of nature has been violated.

The second main issue to address in defending the reality of miracles is the naturalistic bias in the modernist approach. Hume and similarly minded thinkers, committed as they are to the scientism of the Enlightenment, assume that miracles are inherently improbable. For such, any report of a miracle is bound to meet with skepticism because if anyone would care to investigate the truth of the report, contemporary thinking would require such historical inquiry to employ a naturalistic methodology, which precludes the supernatural. These naturalistic rules of studying history were put in place long ago by Ernest Troeltsch (1865–

1923). His principle of analogy requires past events to be of the same kind as the present, thereby calling for "the fundamental homogeneity of all historical events."[10] Supernatural events have no chance in such a scheme. But Wolfhart Pannenberg has argued strongly that it is not justifiable to discount all nonanalogous events from history.[11] Following Pannenberg, Moreland and Craig's critique of Troeltsch's approach is accurate. "Properly defined, analogy means that in a situation that is unclear, the facts ought to be understood in terms of known experience; but Troeltsch has elevated the principle to constrict all past events to purely naturalistic events. But that an event bursts all analogies cannot be used to dispute its historicity."[12]

One more area to explore is Hume's views on testimony as they relate to the reality of the miracles reported in the Bible and other possible reports of miracles. Hume's view is based on probabilities. He notes,

> "No testimony is sufficient to establish a miracle.... When anyone tells me that he saw a dead man restored to life I immediately consider myself, whether it be more probable, that this person should either deceive or be deceived, or that the fact, which he relates, should really have happened. I weigh the one miracle against the other ... and always reject the greater miracle."[13]

In Hume's view, the point is that it is always more probable that the testimony to a miracle is false than that the miracle occurred. Hume has attracted the attention of probability theorists by virtue of his approach and several problems have been detected.[14] First, it was realized that if we simply had to weigh the probabilities of an event occurring against that of the reliability of the witness to it we would end up rejecting events that we know could reasonably happen. A frequently used illustration is that of a lottery pick; say the number x is reported on the news by reporter on a reliable news channel. Clearly, the improbability of the event x overwhelms the probability of the witness' or reporter's credibility to a degree that, following Hume, such reports should never be believed. But this is absurd. Second, what is the probability, if the event had not occurred, that it would be reported as it was? In the case of the lottery pick, it would be quite small. Similarly, the probability, for example, that if Jesus had not been raised from the dead the reports of His resurrection would be as we have them would have to be very small. More important is the increase in probability that results from multiple testimonies. It is noted that "the cumulative power of independent witnesses is such that individually they could be *un*reliable more than 50% of the time and yet their testimony combine to make an event of apparently enormous improbability quite probable in light of their testimony."[15] In Jesus' case, the independence of Peter, James, and Saul as witnesses is quite well established.

Theism and the reality of miracles

Modern thinking sees miracles as naturally impossible and therefore denies them. Belief in a personal God (theism), however, argues that through God's actions an event that is naturally impossible can be transformed into a real historical event. From this perspective, a miracle is on the continuum of God's creative and providential (conservation) acts. Only to the extent that one is committed to atheistic principles will miracles be denied. So, how can miracles be possible? First, by exposing the shaky bases on which miracles are denied as discussed above. Second, by affirming the following claims of theism: there is a personal God; He created the universe; He preserves its being; and He is capable of acting freely within it.

Of course, it must be pointed out that in the Bible we find evidence of entities that perform miracles that are counterfeit to those of the Creator God (e.g., Exodus 7:10, 11). Especially in the last days, we are warned of an explosion of spiritualism in which demons, through the performance of counterfeit miracles, will rally the world towards a common rebellion against God and His people (Revelation 16:12–14).

Conclusion

The denial of miracles is a recent phenomenon based on how modernity has chosen to understand the workings of nature and what is possible in it. We have tried to give several reasons why this position is untenable. First, the denial is incoherent based on modernity's own theories of natural law. Second, to deny miracles because they are violations of natural laws defies a commonsense understanding of the nature of laws. Third, the denial of miracles because they are nonanalogous to other events in history is just the evidence of an unjustifiable naturalistic bias. Finally, based on the nature of biblical testimony of miracles, the improbability argument against miracles initiated by Hume has turned out to work in favor of an enhanced probability of biblical miracles. Eventually, however, belief in theism is the ultimate answer to how miracles can be possible.

Kwabena Donkor *is an associate director of the Biblical Research Institute at the Seventh-day Adventist world headquarters in Silver Spring, Maryland. A graduate of Andrews University, he earned his doctorate in systematic theology, affording him an avenue to explore his lifelong interest in the connections between philosophy, science, and religion. Before coming to the General Conference, he was employed at the Ontario Conference as a district pastor for eleven years. He has written scholarly articles for journals, including* Andrews University Seminary Studies *and* Ministry *magazine, and contributed to Millard Erickson et al.,* Reclaiming the Center: Confronting Evangelical Accommodation in Postmodern Times. *He is an avid music lover and writes music at every affordable opportunity. He is a native of Ghana, and he and his wife, Comfort, have two grown children, Afia and Kwasi.*

References

[1] Wayne A. Grudem, *Systematic Theology: An Introduction to Biblical Doctrine* (Grand Rapids, Mich.: Zondervan, 1994), 355.

[2] See J. P. Moreland and William L. Craig, *Philosophical Foundations for a Christian Worldview* (Downers Grove, Ill.: IVP Academic, 2003), 566.

[3] Ibid. Moreland and Craig observe, "But our exposition of divine providence based on God's middle knowledge suggests a category of nonmiraculous, special providence, which is helpful to distinguish. We have in mind here events that are the product of natural causes but whose context is such as to suggest a special divine intervention with regard to their occurrence."

[4] Barnabas Lindars, "Miracle," in *The Westminster Dictionary of Christian Theology*, eds. Alan Richardson and John Bowden (Philadelphia, Pa.: Westminster, 1983), 371.

[5] See Moreland and Craig, *Philosophical Foundations*, 566–568.

[6] Quoted in George Mavrodes, "Miracles," in *The Oxford Handbook of Philosophy of Religion*, ed. William J. Wainwright (New York: Oxford University Press, 2005), 305.

[7] Ibid., 310

[8] See Moreland and Craig, *Philosophical Foundations*, 569.

[9] Mavrodes, "Miracles," 309, 310.

[10] Ernst Troeltsch, quoted in Gerhard Hasel, *Biblical Interpretation Today* (Lincoln, Neb.: College View Printers, 1985), 75.

[11] Wolfhart Pannenberg, "Redemptive Event and History," in *Basic Questions in Theology*, trans. G. H. Kehm (Philadelphia, Pa.: Fortress, 1970), 1:40–50.

[12] Moreland and Craig, *Philosophical Foundations,* 571.

[13] Quoted in Mavrodes, "Miracles," 314. Notice, though, that Hume himself had a high opinion of the value of testimony, for he argued that "there is no species of reasoning more common, more useful, and even necessary in human life, than that which is derived from the testimony of men, and the reports of eye-witnesses and spectators."

[14] See S. L. Zabell, "The Probabilistic Analysis of Testimony," *Journal of Statistical Planning and Inference* 20 (1988): 327–354. Also, John Earman, *Hume's Abject Failure* (Oxford: Oxford University Press, 2000).

[15] Moreland and Craig, *Philosophical Foundations,* 570.

GREG A. KING

Chapter 9

Is the God of the Old Testament Different From the One in the New Testament?

"God is love," declares the apostle John in his first epistle to the early believers (1 John 4:8). For many centuries, Christians have accorded great importance to this brief declaration. They have understood it to express the primary defining characteristic of God. They have taken this little phrase to highlight who God is at the core of His being, to set forth His foremost quality. And since the Bible affirms the unchanging nature of God (Malachi 3:6), Christians have generally stated that God's love is on display throughout Scripture—in the Old Testament as well as the New.

The problem

However, not all people agree that the entire Bible portrays a loving God. In his recent best-selling book, militant atheist Richard Dawkins pulls no punches when he asserts, "The God of the Old Testament is arguably the most unpleasant character in all fiction: jealous and proud of it; a petty, unjust, unforgiving control-freak; a vindictive, bloodthirsty ethnic cleanser; a misogynistic, homophobic, racist, infanticidal, genocidal, filicidal, pestilential, megalomaniacal, sadomasochistic, capriciously malevolent bully."[1] To say the least (and much more could be said about Dawkins and his book), Dawkins does not see the Old Testament as describing a God of love.

And it's not just atheists who are challenged by the Old Testament's description of God. Many casual readers of the Bible, and even a number of Christians, struggle with the Old Testament God. It appears to them, at least on the surface, that the description of God in the Old Testament presents a striking and dramatic contrast with that found in the New. Their impression is that the God of the Old Testament is harsh, vindictive, and punitive, while the New Testament God—as shown in Jesus Christ—reveals Himself as loving, gracious, and merciful.

How should this issue be engaged? Are there some responses that support the orthodox Christian position that the Bible's portrayal of God is unified and consistent, that God is a God of love in both the Old Testament and the New? Or is the chasm between the descriptions of God in the Old and New Testaments so great and yawning that they cannot be bridged?

Solutions to the problem

We will discuss some points that move the discussion of this challenging issue in a positive direction and provide some help in understanding it. However, first it is appropriate to review several solutions that have been advocated and popularly held but that can be judged as inadequate or erroneous on the basis of Scripture, even though they may have attracted a wide following.

Unacceptable solutions

One solution, advocated by Marcion in the second century A.D., is simply to state that the God of the Old Testament is different from the God of the New Testament. According to Marcion, the God of the New Testament, the heavenly Father who sent Jesus and whom Jesus preached about, is kind, merciful, and forgiving. By contrast, the Old Testament God, the Creator of the material universe, is a jealous tribal Deity whose law demands justice and who punishes people for their sins. In light of his view, it is not surprising that Marcion rejected the entire Old Testament and accepted a limited number of New Testament books that he had edited to favor his perspective.

However, Marcion was correctly judged a heretic and disfellowshiped by the early church, and there are compelling reasons why his perspective must be rejected. First, throughout the New Testament, it is assumed that the God who "so loved the world" (John 3:16, NIV) that He gave His Son to die is the same God as the God of the Old Testament. Additionally, Jesus Himself is identified as the active Agent in Creation, the One who brought all things into existence (John 1:3, 14), not some evil deity as Marcion contended. It is a telling and decisive point that Jesus never distances Himself either from the God of the Old Testament or the Old Testament Scriptures. Rather, He saw His life in continuity with and in fulfillment of the Old Testament (Luke 24:27, 44).

Another suggestion that doesn't go as far as Marcion's heresy is that the same God is present in the Old and New Testaments but that He has a split personality. That is to say, God dealt with people differently in Old Testament times than in the New Testament era. Those who advocate this solution think that for some reason God chose to act harshly and punitively in His dealings with the Israelites and other nations in the Old Testament, but with the dawn of the New Testament, God's gentleness and kindness come to the forefront.

This previous suggestion is developed in a rather elaborate way and given a veneer of sophistication in the theological system known as dispensationalism. Rooted in the nineteenth-century writings of John Darby and popularized in the marginal notes of the Scofield Reference Bible, which had a wide distribution, dispensationalism continues to be a widely held view among many American Christians. It maintains that God has related to people in different ways through a series of different dispensations or periods of time down through history. For example, Adam and Eve's time in Eden was the dispensation of innocence, the pre-Flood world was the dispensation of conscience, and the majority of the Old Testament era was the dispensation of law. It also holds that these different dispensations are based on different biblical covenants.

However, dispensationalism, like Marcion's view, falters on the grounds of the obvious continuity that is seen between God and His dealings in both Testaments. In fact, God declares of Himself, "I the Lord do not change" (Malachi 3:6, NIV).

Helpful solutions

What are some points to consider that might help us understand the Old Testament portrayal of God and bridge the gap that is sometimes thought to exist between the God of the Old Testament and the God of the New Testament as revealed by Jesus?

The first point worth noting is that Jesus never distanced Himself from the God of the Old Testament. Never does He make a statement

Is the God of the Old Testament Different From the One in the New Testament?

even hinting that His character or teachings are distinct and separate from the Old Testament revelation of God. He certainly distinguished His viewpoint and teachings from Jewish traditional understandings on a variety of topics (Matthew 5:21, 22, 27, 28, 31, 32; 15:1–11), but never did He depart from what the Old Testament reveals about God. To the contrary, it was the Old Testament God who gave Him to the world out of love (John 3:16), and He came as Immanuel, "God with us" (Matthew 1:23, NIV; quoting Isaiah 7:14), as the living embodiment of the Old Testament God. Since Jesus didn't separate the revelation of God provided by His life from the Old Testament God, as His followers we should not do so either.

A second point worth making is that, if one takes Scripture seriously, God is not a one-dimensional Deity, with love as His only attribute. Rather, a number of characteristics are attributed to the Divine Person. He is holy, righteous, just, faithful, jealous, merciful, and gracious, and so on. Quite a long list of biblical attributes could be adduced, and to eliminate aspects of the biblical descriptions of God because they don't fit in with our concept of a God of love is to engage in reductionism. Such an exercise would leave us with a diminished picture of God that is unfaithful to Scripture. We must let the Bible define the character and ways of God instead of deciding what God must be like and then imposing our view onto Scripture.

A third point to keep in mind is that the New Testament, like the Old, contains some challenging passages when it comes to understanding the character of God. In other words, the God of the New Testament, even as seen in Jesus Christ, is not always a warm, fuzzy God who is gentle in every circumstance.

Several biblical passages serve to demonstrate this point. First, the divine judgment that took the lives of Ananias and Sapphira for lying to the Holy Spirit is certainly a serious punishment (Acts 5:1–11). Some might even view this as a vestige of the harsh Old Testament God, though it is found in the New Testament. The New Testament's final book speaks of a judgment from God that contains undiluted wrath, a divine anger that is unmixed with mercy (Revelation 14:9–11). Also, Jesus Himself drove the merchants out of the temple with a whip of cords (John 2:13–17) and initially rebuffed the plea of a Canaanite woman for healing for her daughter with what some consider to be a pejorative comment (Matthew 15:21–28). All of this is not to deny that the New Testament God is infinitely gracious and loving; it is simply to note that both Old and New Testaments at times present challenges as we seek to understand the loving ways of God.

A fourth point to keep in mind is the concept that Christians sometimes refer to as progressive revelation. Progressive revelation refers to the gradual unfolding of truth, to the fact that as we move through Scripture God reveals Himself and His character more and more clearly until we reach the apex of His self-revelation in the person of His Son, Jesus Christ. This is not to say that the revelation of God found in the Old Testament is erroneous and mistaken. It is certainly the case that David, Isaiah, Daniel, and other Old Testament writers received insights about God and communicated them in the pages of Scripture. However, it is an incomplete revelation.

As the Bible indicates, the fullest revelation of God is found in the life of His Son, Jesus Christ. No Old Testament prophet could ever say, as did Jesus, "He who has seen Me has seen the Father" (John 14:9, NASB).

Is the God of the Old Testament Different From the One in the New Testament?

Jesus is the only One of whom it could be said, "For in him dwelleth all the fulness of the Godhead bodily" (Colossians 2:9, KJV). For that matter, we must remember that as long as we are on this earth, even with the wonderful disclosure of God provided by Jesus, we will still, to use the words of Paul, "see in a mirror dimly" (1 Corinthians 13:12, NASB). Only in eternity will we begin to understand some of the challenges to our understanding of God posed by certain passages in Scripture.

A final point to keep in mind is that our unease and squeamishness about the Old Testament description of God might tell us more about the world in which we live and about us than it does about God. Perhaps our age prefers a God whose affection is indulgent and permissive instead of One whose love is holy and jealous (Exodus 20:5; 34:14). Maybe we desire a Lord who is warm and cozy instead of One who is, as the New Testament declares, "a consuming fire" (Hebrews 12:29, NASB).

The following quotation from C. S. Lewis is a striking indictment of our age:

> What would really satisfy us would be a God who said of anything we happened to like doing, "What does it matter so long as they are contented?" We want, in fact, not so much a Father in Heaven as a grandfather in heaven—a senile benevolence who, as they say, "liked to see young people enjoying themselves," and whose plan for the universe was simply that it might be truly said at the end of each day, "a good time was had by all."[2]

Instead of limiting ourselves to God's revelation of Himself in only one portion of Scripture, let us follow the example of many faithful

Christians, the New Testament apostles, and Jesus Himself. May we recognize the continuity in the Word of God, and plumb the depths of the entirety of the Bible, seeking to understand as completely and fully as possible the One whom to know is life eternal (John 17:3).

For further reading:

Baker, David. *Two Testaments, One Bible: The Theological Relationship Between the Old and New Testaments.* Downers Grove, Ill.: IVP Academic, 2010.

Baylis, Albert. *From Creation to the Cross: Understanding the First Half of the Bible.* Grand Rapids, Mich.: Zondervan, 1996.

Dybdahl, Jon. *A Strange Place for Grace: Discovering a Loving God in the Old Testament.* Nampa, Idaho: Pacific Press®, 2006.

Yancey, Philip. *The Bible Jesus Read.* Grand Rapids, Mich.: Zondervan, 1999.

Greg A. King is dean of the School of Religion and professor of biblical studies at Southern Adventist University. In addition to his theology degree from Southern, he has degrees from the Adventist Theological Seminary and Union Theological Seminary in Virginia, where he earned his doctorate in Old Testament. He has written for a number of publications, such as the Eerdmans Dictionary of the Bible, Bibliotheca Sacra, Andrews University Seminary Studies, Ministry, *and the* Adventist Review. *Additionally, he authored the book* Kings and Chronicles. *Prior to teaching, he did pastoral work in Tennessee, Georgia, and Iowa. He and his wife, Mary, have two sons, Jonathan and Joshua. His real passion in life is to see all of his students develop a living, vibrant relationship with Jesus Christ so that they might experience the abundant life made possible by this connection.*

References

[1] Richard Dawkins, *The God Delusion* (Boston: Houghton Mifflin, 2008), 31.

[2] C. S. Lewis, *The Problem of Pain* (New York: Macmillan, 1962), 40.

JOHN W. REEVE

Chapter 10

How Is It That We Do Not Worship Three Gods?

The conception of God as Trinity has always been both central and problematic to Christianity. Nevertheless, "Three Persons in One God" effectively summarizes biblical revelation about the nature of the Godhead. Externally, this conceptualization of God has caused the other two monotheistic religions, Judaism and Islam, to accuse Christianity of being polytheistic. Internally, ever since the early Christian church chose this Trinitarian formula to best express what the Bible revealed about God, no doctrine has seemed more essential to the Christian conceptualization of God.[1] At the same time, the doctrine of the Trinity has been repeatedly attacked as an illogical misrepresentation of God by various determined minorities.

Adventists and Trinitarianism

In early nineteenth-century America, the Christian Connection, a small denomination, which for a time counted Joseph Bates and James White among its ministers, was one such anti-Trinitarian minority. As leaders in the little flock that grew and eventually organized into the Seventh-day Adventist Church, Bates and White contributed to an anti-Trinitarian overtone in the formative years of the movement. Over time, however, this early aversion to Trinitarian theology was replaced with the recognition that though the Scriptures do not use the term *Trinity*, the descriptions of God given in Scripture call for such a conception.[2] During the 1890s, when the Adventist understanding of Jesus Christ heightened and *The Desire of Ages* was written, most Seventh-day Adventists came to a Trinitarian understanding of God as Father, Son, and Holy Spirit.[3]

A healthy process caused many early Adventist leaders to initially reject the traditional doctrine of the Trinity. They viewed this doctrine as coming from tradition rather than from the Bible. Furthermore, some of them confused the Trinitarian formula of Three Persons in One God with the modalistic conceptualization of God as One Person in three modes. Joseph Bates wrote that he could never accept that Jesus Christ and the Father were one and the same Person.[4] This initial rejection set a healthy hermeneutic of not accepting Christian tradition as authoritative, but instead, only accepting doctrine as they understood it from the Bible. Thus, when the Seventh-day Adventist Church did turn to a Trinitarian understanding of God, it was because they believed it to be the best representation of all that the Scriptures revealed about God.

Such a shift in the conception of God has implications for how one relates to God, and also how one perceives salvation. Viewing God as a heavenly Trio of Three equal Persons making up a single Godhead has far-reaching ramifications for the doctrines of Christ, the Holy Spirit, and salvation.

Revelation and logic

That three are one is a logical impossibility. It defies mathematical logic; it also defies Aristotelian logic. So why did the early church conceptualize God as Three in One?

First, and most simply, it was because the writers of the New Testament so clearly portrayed Jesus Christ as God along with the Father. Nearly every salutation or praise includes God the Father and the Lord Jesus Christ in conjunction (Romans 1:7; 1 Corinthians 1:1–3; 2 Corinthians 1:2; Ephesians 1:3–6; Philippians 2:5–11; James 1:1; 1 Peter 1:2; 2 John 3; Jude 25; Revelation 1:9). Further exploration of the biblical teaching finds both the oneness and the threeness of God in Scripture. The oneness is clear in passages such as Deuteronomy 6:4, which the Jews use in the *Shema,* "Hear oh Israel, the Lord our God, the Lord is one."[5] The threeness can be seen in passages such as the baptism of Christ in Matthew 3:16, 17, where the Father, the Son, and the Spirit are individually described as simultaneously active. It is also evident in the Great Commission in Matthew 28:19, where Jesus commands His disciples to make disciples and baptize them "in the name of the Father and the Son and the Holy Spirit" (NASB),[6] which became the standard benediction in the Christian church. Thus, two great prayers from the Bible, the *Shema* and the benediction, describe God as One and as Three.

In spite of human logic, the Bible insists that God is One and that God is Three. So, do we give priority to human logic or revelation?

Trinity: Solution or paradox?

Expressed this starkly, I will follow revelation before logic. Any other answer creates a theology built from the bottom up, a human understanding based on perception and analogy. On the other hand, placing divine revelation before logic allows for a theology revealed from above, from the self-revelation of God, who is infinitely greater and wiser than human minds can conceive. Granted, this revelation comes through human agents and human language so that we are but "seeing through a glass darkly" and "knowing in part" (1 Corinthians 13:12); yet I would rather partially see the true God, who is far above human conception, than to claim a full view of a humanly constructed Divinity.

The Trinitarian formula is summarized simply: God is Three and God is One: Triune equals Trinity. The concepts are straightforward and biblical; the term is simply a name signifying that which God reveals about Himself in the Scriptures.

The early church did not resolve the revealed paradox that God is One, and yet God is Three.[7] They simply *named* it.

Trinity is not a solution. It is simply a one-word designation that holds the paradox intact: Three in One, our Triune God.[8]

The Holy Spirit as a personal Member of the Godhead

There is an assertion that floats around that the Holy Spirit is not a personal Member of the Godhead, but an impersonal power from God. This assertion, which has a small following in Adventism, takes many forms and angles, but at its core it asserts that the Bible does not support a view of the Holy Spirit as having any "personhood." I will address the issue directly from the Bible, which, if it gives strong evidence for ascribing personhood and full deity to the Holy Spirit, settles the question for me. Afterward, I will address one historical and one philosophical idea that may shed light on the perceived confusion concerning the Holy Spirit.

The first category I will address is interpersonal relationship. In his closing address to his letters to the Corinthians, Paul initiated a classical Trinitarian benediction: "May the grace of the Lord Jesus Christ, and the love of God, and the fellowship of the Holy Spirit be with you all" (2 Corinthians 13:14, NIV). Here Paul recognizes that the Holy Spirit is especially identified with fellowship (*koinonia*), which is the very heart of interpersonal relationship. Other Scriptures describe the personal ministry that the Holy Spirit undertakes in direct relation to individual believers. These include convicting (John 16:8–11), regenerating (John 3:5–8), guiding (John 16:13), sanctifying (Romans 8:1–17), empowering for service (Acts 1:8), revealing (Luke 2:26), and moving the inspired prophets to speak and write the Scriptures (2 Timothy 3:16; 2 Peter 1:21). All these denote an active or relational function. Even when the Spirit is portrayed as not asserting His own will (as in "He will not speak on His own initiative" [John 16:13, NASB]), there is an active relational component in the description of personal relationship to the believer (as in the same verse "He will guide," "He will speak; and He will disclose"). The texts in 2 Timothy 3:16 and 2 Peter 1:21, along with numerous texts describing being filled with the Holy Spirit, denote that the Holy Spirit is responsible for the production of Scripture and prophecy, which have propositional content. This task, like all those listed above, involves more than impersonal power; it requires the conscious communication of content. All these personal interactions with individual believers highlight what Paul pointed out at the end of the Corinthian letters: the Holy Spirit is in an especially close personal relationship/fellowship/*koinonia* with us.

In John 14–17, we find the Father, Son, and Spirit portrayed as being in an interdependent interactive relationship for the purpose of including us in Their intimate, reciprocal relationship of love and obedience. If you see and know the Son, you see and know the Father (14:6, 9); the Son reveals the Father (17:6, 25); and while the Son brings glory to the Father, the Father glorifies the Son (17:4). The Father sends the Son (16:5) and the Spirit (14:26); the Son sends the Spirit (15:26; 16:7); the Spirit teaches, guides, and testifies concerning the Son (14:25; 15:26); and through the Spirit living in us, the Son, who is in the Father, will come to us (14:16–20). The interactions are portrayed as reciprocal among all Three. This is especially true as pictured in chapter 17, verses 6–10: Through the revelation of the Father by the Son to us—who are described as being given to the Son by the Father—the Son gains trust to give us the words the Father gave to Him, and to enable us to accept those words in obedience. In this way, the Son is a bridge between the Father and us, as believers, engendering the loving, trusting, believing, and obeying intimate relationship. This bridge of the Son is secured to us forever by the Spirit living in us (14:16–18). True, the Son and the Spirit take submissive roles in this relationship for our salvation (14:31), but there is another aspect of these verses that tend to suggest equality: unity.

The Gospel of John contains several direct statements of unity between the Father and the Son: "I am in the Father, and the Father is in me" (14:10, NIV); "All I have is yours, and all you have is mine" (17:10, NIV); even a direct "we are one" (17:22, NIV). This unity extends indirectly to the Spirit as well, as evidenced in John 16:14, 15: The Spirit "will bring glory to me by taking from what is mine and making it known to you. All that belongs to the Father is mine. That is why I said the Spirit will take from what is mine and make it known to you" (NIV). This reciprocal ownership and open access to what the Three share describes a unity of the Three. Similarly, John 14:16–23 portrays a unified indwelling. Though He had to leave us, Jesus indicates that He will come to us through the promise of the Spirit living in us. Then, Jesus finishes the passage with the promise that He and the Father both will come to us and make Their home in us. This Father and Son making Their home in us is on account of the Spirit living in us. This is a strong unity that equates the presence of One of the Three with the presence of all Three.

Whether this unity is perceived as a unity of purpose or a unity of being has been hotly contested, but either way the unity of the Three is a perception of a Trinity. This unity of the Three also suggests that the Holy Spirit has personhood just as the Father and the Son have personhood. That, along with the clear interpersonal relationship that the Spirit has with the believers, strongly suggests that the Bible presents the Holy Spirit as a Person, even though most biblical presentations of the Spirit do not include a body. Personhood is not derived from a body but from a relationship.

How did the Holy Spirit begin to be understood as an impersonal force? The answer lies in history and philosophy. The philosophical milieu of the early Christians included a Platonic and Stoic conception of God in three parts: The transcendent One, or *Monad,* which Plato called the "Father"; the demiurge or Logos who was the immanent Creator, which Plato sometimes referred to as the *Dyad* (Two) or as the "Son"; and the infusive power of life and energy that fills all the universe and the living creatures in it with life force and power, which Plato and Zeno of Citium called the *Pneuma,* that is "breath" or "spirit." This philosophical conception of spirit was often assumed when reading Scriptures about the

Holy Spirit, thereby tending to make the traditional readings of Scripture emphasize the subordinate role of the Spirit and using verbiage that could construe the Spirit as only a force. The texts that portray the personal and relational aspects of the Spirit initially received less use and theological weight. However, neither philosophy nor tradition should control our readings of Scripture.

Ramifications for salvation concerning the tri-unity of God

So far we have seen an overview of the development of the biblical doctrine of the Trinity—both in the early Christian centuries and in the Seventh-day Adventist Church—addressed the paradox of Three in One, and seen the Holy Spirit as a full personal Member of the Godhead. Now we will turn our attention to the ramifications of the saving relationship with our God as Three Persons within the One Godhead. The core of those ramifications is that our salvation is secured by the very God who is the Creator and Sustainer of all. Jesus Christ is God!

In John 1, we have a description of Jesus Christ as the Logos (Word). This Word is described as both Creator and God (verses 1–3), the all-powerful Ruler of the universe (see Titus 2:11–14, where Paul describes Christ as "our great God," and Romans 9:5, where He is the "eternally blessed God" [NKJV]). Most Adventists would be familiar with Ellen White's description of Jesus Christ as "one in nature, in character, in purpose" with God the Father.[9] John 1 describes that nature and character of God as life and light (verses 4, 5), emphasizing that the Word is the Source of both eternal life and eternal truth. In verse 14, John says that this "Word became flesh and dwelt among us" (NKJV), summarizing the Christmas story, in which the great, eternal God becomes a helpless child. Growing and becoming aware of His mission as the Messiah, He carries on a public ministry for some three years while preaching the kingdom of God and preparing His disciples for His death. Then He died, as a sacrifice, the Passover lamb, the Suffering Servant by whose stripes we are healed (Isaiah 53; especially verses 5–10). However, He did not stay dead! As He said, "I have authority to lay it down [my life and] . . . authority to take it up again" (John 10:18, NIV). This brings to mind that oft-quoted passage of Ellen White: "In Christ is life, original, unborrowed, underived. . . . The divinity of Christ is the believer's assurance of eternal life."[10]

    I cannot but honor such a God.

    God the Son, in His role as Savior (1) is the Almighty, (2) loves us, and (3) is Himself the bridge of salvation connecting us humans back to God. Only the true God can accomplish these three tasks of our salvation. If He were less than fully divine, His ability to save would be diminished. To view Him as less than fully divine diminishes our ability to comprehend and enjoy His work of salvation. As John 15:13 declares, "No one has greater love than this, that [he] would lay down his life for his friends" (HCSB).

    I cannot but love such a God.

For further reading:

Erickson, Millard. *Making Sense of the Trinity: Three Crucial Questions*. Grand Rapids, Mich.: Baker, 2000.

"The Mission of the Holy Spirit," in *Seventh-day Adventists Believe*. 2nd ed. Nampa, Idaho: Pacific Press®, 2005, 73–77.

Wallenkampf, Arnold. *New by the Spirit*. Reissued. Hagerstown, Md.: Review and Herald®, 2006.

Whidden, Woodrow, Jerry Moon, and John Reeve. *The Trinity: Understanding God's Love, His Plan of Salvation, and Christian Relationships*. Hagerstown, Md.: Review and Herald®, 2002.

John W. Reeve received his PhD from the University of Notre Dame and is an assistant professor of church history at the Seventh-day Adventist Theological Seminary at Andrews University. He is the editor of Andrews University Seminary Studies. *He is also the coauthor of* The Trinity, *where his chapters outline the development of the doctrine of the Trinity in the early Christian church through the Middle Ages. His first teaching experience was at the secondary level in British Columbia, where he started Our Daily Bread Bakery. After completing his MDiv, his pastoral experience was in the Minnesota Conference. His wife, Teresa L. Reeve, PhD, is an assistant professor of New Testament in the Adventist Theological Seminary at Berrien Springs, Michigan, where they live with their daughter, Madeleine.*

References

[1] See my three chapters on the early history of the Trinity doctrine in *The Trinity: Understanding God's Love, His Plan of Salvation, and Christian Relationships* (Hagerstown, Md.: Review and Herald®, 2002), 124–160. For an audio presentation, listen to my "The Trinity in the Early Centuries" podcast at www.atsjats.org/article.php?id=33#3. For more details, see R. P. Hanson, *The Search for the Christian Doctrine of God* (Edinburgh: Clark, 1988).

[2] Jerry Moon, "The Adventist Trinity Debate, Part 1: Historical Overview," *Andrews University Seminary Studies* 41 (2003): 113–129; Merlin Burt, "History of Seventh-day Adventist Views on the Trinity," *Journal of the Adventist Theological Society* 17 (2006): 125–139.

³ Jerry Moon, "The Adventist Trinity Debate, Part 2: The Role of Ellen G. White," *Andrews University Seminary Studies* 41 (2003): 275–292.

⁴ Joseph Bates, *Autobiography of Elder Joseph Bates* (Battle Creek, Mich.: Steam Press, 1868), 205. Cf. Merlin Burt, "The Trinity in Seventh-day Adventist History," *Ministry*, February 2009, 5–8; George Knight, *Joseph Bates: The Real Founder of Seventh-day Adventism* (Hagerstown, Md.: Review and Herald®, 2004), 38.

⁵ Monotheism is a strong concept in the whole Bible. Many other biblical passages emphasize the oneness of God (Mark 12:29; John 5:44; Romans 3:30; 1 Corinthians 8:4, 6; Galatians 3:20; Ephesians 4:6; James 2:19), or allude to the oneness of God (Joshua 22:22; 1 Samuel 2:2; Psalms 50:1; 71:22; Isaiah 46:9; Malachi 2:10), or declare the exclusiveness of God as the only God (1 Kings 8:60; 2 Chronicles 14:11).

⁶ Other texts of the New Testament name Two or even all Three of the Members of the Godhead in conjunction with each other (John 3:5; Acts 2:38; 7:55; 10:38; Romans 1:4; 8:9; 15:16, 30; 1 Corinthians 6:11; 2 Corinthians 3:3; 13:14; Galatians 3:14; 4:6; Ephesians 2:18; 4:6; Philippians 3:3; Hebrews 9:14; 1 Peter 1:2; 2:5; 3:18; 4:14; Revelation 19:10).

⁷ To try to explain *how* God can be both Three and One goes beyond the simplest expression, and becomes more complex and metaphorical. However, we do not always need to explain how in order to believe what the Bible clearly teaches. The simplest explanation is to say that God is One God in Three Persons. This is a very useful conceptualization, but it has its drawbacks. The English term *person* is used here in approximation of two Greek terms: *prosopon*, meaning face, mask, personality, role; and *hypostasis*, which has a wide semantic field including personality, character, or more directly, nature. The Latin term *persona*, meaning personality, character, role, does not have the exact same semantic field as the English *person* or either of the above Greek terms that were used through history to describe the *how* of the threeness represented in Scripture. Thus, the English term *person* is both helpful, but also can be a hindrance in conceptualizing the individuation within the Godhead as being like we individual human persons are. In a very real sense, any explanation of how God is Three in One must be seen as portraying the concept rather than as an exact description. That God is Three in One is clearly revealed in Scripture; describing how this is so is human construction, and therefore only an approximation. The basic doctrine of the Trinity stands from Scripture whether or not an acceptable approximation of "how" is reached.

⁸ Through the centuries, many ideas have become attached to the basic Trinitarian conceptualizations, as inquisitive Christians attempted to be more and more exact in their constructions of how God is Three in One and of the relationships among the Persons of the Godhead. Some of these are conceptually misleading or used in a misleading way. An example of this can be seen in the conceptualization of the eternal generation of the Son and the eternal procession of the Holy Spirit (that the Son and the Spirit have always been, yet are always coming from the Father). These have been described recently by Thomas Torrance (*Trinitarian Perspectives* [Edinburgh: Clark, 1994], 112, 113, 118, 119) as a necessary part of explaining the eternal relations within the Godhead, yet in no way entailing subordination because the generation and procession is from the *Monarchy* (God's rulership) rather than from the Person of the Father. Some may think it is necessary to use this explanation in order to emphasize the conception of the unity or oneness of God, but it causes conceptual complexity and suggests potential subordinationism. As well, it depends on a Platonic view of eternal timelessness preceding Creation. Various conceptions of a tripartite human corresponding to the threeness in the Trinity I also find misleading. These things are not absolutely

connected with the basic conceptualization of the Trinity. Some Christians may deem all of these as necessary to Trinitarian dogma, but I disagree, for Scripture does not insist on them. These additional ideas are not found in the fundamental beliefs of the Seventh-day Adventist Church.

[9] Ellen G. White, *Patriarchs and Prophets* (Washington, D.C.: Review and Herald®, 1958), 34.

[10] White, *The Desire of Ages* (Mountain View, Calif.: Pacific Press®, 1940), 530.

WERNER K. VYHMEISTER

Chapter 11

What's So Special About the Seventh Day of the Week?

The seventh day of the week appears numerous times in the Bible, from Genesis to Revelation, as a significant component of God's plan and as an indication of divine interest in the life of human beings. It is called the "seventh day" (Genesis 2:2) and also the "Sabbath" (beginning with Exodus 16:23). The seven-day week appears early in biblical history as a unit of time measurement (cf. Genesis 7:4, 10; 8:10, 12; 29:27).

Entire books have been written to discuss the meaning of the Sabbath and its fascinating history during the past millennia. What follows is a brief survey of Sabbath-day highlights, from Genesis to Revelation. This survey tells us why the Sabbath is special.

God Himself rested during the seventh day of Creation week (Genesis 2:2)

Obviously, God was not tired. Nor were Adam and Eve, created just the previous day. But God chose to show them His love and care from the very beginning. *Millennia before the Israelites emerged as a nation,*

God wanted to make clear that the seventh-day Sabbath was made for all humankind, just as Jesus pointed out in Mark 2:27: "The Sabbath was made for man, and not man for the Sabbath."[1]

God blessed the seventh day and sanctified it (Genesis 2:3)

On purpose, God made the Sabbath doubly special by *blessing* it and by *sanctifying* it (Genesis 2:3). There is no biblical reference to any other day of the week that has been blessed or sanctified by God.

The Sabbath commandment, which prescribes that the Sabbath be remembered "to keep it holy" (Exodus 20:8), together with the other nine, is part of the only known document written by God's own finger on the tablets of stone. These tablets were eventually placed inside the ark, in the Most Holy Place of the sanctuary (Exodus 25:16, 21) and, later on, in Solomon's temple (2 Kings 8:9), thus showing the sanctity of the day and of the law that commanded its keeping.

Centuries later, Isaiah (eighth to seventh centuries B.C.) would remind Judah:

> "If because of the sabbath, you turn your foot
> From doing your own pleasure on My holy day,
> And call the sabbath a delight, the holy day of the LORD honorable,
> And shall honor it, desisting from your own ways,
> From seeking your own pleasure,
> And speaking your own word,
> Then you will take delight in the LORD" (Isaiah 58:13, 14).

Through the ages, God considered the Sabbath holy, an extension, as it were, of His own holiness to be shared by His people on earth. Its holiness appears in the Pentateuch (Leviticus 23:3; Deuteronomy 5:12), in the prophets (Jeremiah 17:24, 27; Ezekiel 44:24), and in the history of the Jewish people after their return to Palestine following the Babylonian captivity (Nehemiah 9:14; 13:22).

In different ways, through the following millennia, God emphasized correct Sabbath observance as a sign of loyalty

Even before Israel arrived at Mount Sinai, God began to provide the daily manna (Exodus 16:2–31). It appeared on the ground every morning, except for the Sabbath. On the sixth day, a double portion of manna was provided. For the forty years of wilderness travel, until they crossed the Jordan River into Canaan (Joshua 5:12), the manna helped the Israelites as a weekly reminder of God's loving care and of proper Sabbath observance.

The Levitical sanctuary service included features that highlighted the special character of the weekly Sabbath. It was the only day set for a regular holy, weekly convocation: "For six days work may be done, but on the seventh day there is a sabbath of complete rest, a holy convocation. You shall not do any work; it is a sabbath to the Lord in all your dwellings" (Leviticus 23:3). Only on Sabbath a second lamb was added to both morning and evening sacrifices (Numbers 28:3, 4, 9, 10).

According to Ezekiel 20:12 (590 b.c.), the weekly Sabbath was given as a sign between God and the people of Israel, "that they might know that I am the Lord who sanctifies them."

An important element in Nehemiah's mission (fifth century B.C.) in Judah was the restoration of proper (seventh-day) Sabbath observance (cf. Nehemiah 13:15–22). This included closing down the gates of Jerusalem "as it grew dark . . . before the sabbath" to keep the merchants out "until after the sabbath" (Nehemiah 13:19). It was a reminder of the story of Creation: each day begins with the "evening" (at sundown) and is followed by the "morning" (Genesis 1).

The Sabbath is a memorial of Creation

The fourth commandment, as presented in Exodus 20, gives the reason for keeping the Sabbath: "For in six days the LORD made the heavens and the earth, the sea and all that is in them" (verse 11). In Exodus 31:17, the commandment reiterates the creatorship of God manifested in Sabbath observance: "It is a sign between Me and the sons of Israel forever; for in six days the LORD made heaven and earth, but on the seventh day He ceased from labor, and was refreshed."

In his seminal book on the Sabbath, early Adventist pioneer J. N. Andrews writes of the importance of Sabbath keeping and is quoted by Ellen White: " 'The importance of the Sabbath as a memorial of creation is that it keeps ever present the true reason why worship is due to God. . . . The Sabbath therefore lies at the very foundation of divine worship, for it teaches this great truth in the most impressive manner, and no other institution does this.' "[2] Ellen White quotes this passage from Andrews and then reflects, "Had the Sabbath been universally kept, man's thoughts and affections would have been led to the Creator as the object of reverence and worship, and there would never have been an idolater, an atheist, or an infidel. The keeping of the Sabbath is a sign of loyalty to the true God."[3]

Jesus Christ highlighted the significance of the weekly Sabbath

Christ's custom was to attend the synagogue on the Sabbath and to actively participate in the worship service. Early in His ministry, on a Sabbath in Nazareth, He read from the book of Isaiah and then announced, "Today this Scripture has been fulfilled in your hearing" (Luke 4:16–21).

The gospel record includes seven "deeds of mercy" (miracles) that were performed by Jesus on the seventh-day Sabbath. In the synagogue at Capernaum, Jesus cast out a demon (Mark 1:21–31). On another Sabbath, Jesus healed a man with a withered hand in the synagogue, causing turmoil among the observers (Mark 3:1–5). Luke relates the healing of a woman who had been bent over for eighteen years, causing the indignation of the synagogue official; Christ defended His action, noting that it was appropriate that she should be loosed from her bond on the Sabbath (Luke 13:10–17). To respond to the query of the Pharisees and lawyers, "Is it lawful to heal on the Sabbath, or not?" Jesus healed a man suffering from dropsy (Luke 14:1–4). The story of the man who had been ill for thirty-eight years, whom Jesus healed at the pool of Bethesda on a Sabbath, is reported in John 5:1–15. According to John 9:1–7, Jesus made clay and anointed the eyes of one blind from birth on the Sabbath. All of these miracles caused sensation, but they gave Jesus the opportunity to declare Himself "Lord even of the Sabbath" (Mark 2:28) and to point to the restorative nature of the Sabbath.

Very close to the end of His earthly ministry, in the prophetic sermon recorded in Matthew 24, Jesus alerted His followers about events that would take place in the not-so-distant future, when the "ABOMINATION of desolation" would stand in the Holy Place, signifying the fall of Jerusalem to the Roman armies. He urged them to pray that their flight might "not be in the winter, or on a Sabbath." In His loving foresight, He did not wish His followers to suffer from the rigors of the Judean winter. He also intended to let them know that the Sabbath would still be valid (Matthew 24:15–17, 20).

Even in death, Jesus rested in the tomb on the Sabbath, beginning before sundown on Friday (John 19:38–42; cf. also 20:1–18). The gospel story clearly indicates that His followers likewise rested that fateful Sabbath: "And on the Sabbath they rested according to the commandment" (Luke 23:56).

The apostles kept the seventh-day Sabbath

After Christ's ascension, the apostles continued to keep the seventh-day Sabbath as Christian congregations developed throughout the territory of the Roman Empire, and beyond. Among the first converts, there were Jews of the Diaspora and also local Gentiles.

Specific reference is made to the Sabbath meetings of Paul and his associates with Jews and "Greek" proselytes in Pisidian Antioch (Acts 13), Philippi (Acts 16), Thessalonica (Acts 17), and Corinth (Acts 18).

All New Testament writers appear to teach (explicitly or implicitly) that the Ten Commandments given by God at Mount Sinai (including the fourth) were still valid. But John saw in vision how Satan, for 1,260 years, was going to persecute the church, those "who keep the commandments of God and hold to the testimony of Jesus" (Revelation 12:1–17; cf. also Daniel 7).

True, there is reference to a gathering in Troas "to break bread" on the first day of the week (Acts 20:7–11). On that night, as the meeting ran long, Eutychus fell out of the window to his death; Paul brought him back to life. By daybreak, the meeting was over and Paul left. Nothing is said about this event as the celebration of any kind of Sabbath service.

The Sabbath is a token of the rest—now and eternally— that believers in Christ may have

Hebrews 4 goes into detail about the rest that God offered to human beings from the first Sabbath of this world's history. The rest given to Israel when they entered Canaan was another aspect of God's great rest. Believers could enter into this rest, just as God rested from His creative work. And the author of Hebrews called this rest *sabbatismós*—a Sabbath rest. The rest and peace of salvation are symbolized by the weekly Sabbath rest—a scrap of time that points to the rest offered by Jesus, who invited us all: "Come to Me, all who are weary and heavy-laden, and I will give you rest. Take My yoke upon you, and learn from Me, for I am gentle and humble in heart; and YOU SHALL FIND REST FOR YOUR SOULS" (Matthew 11:28, 29).

To summarize, What's so special about the seventh day of the week?

Much could be said. Let's highlight the following:

1. God created the Sabbath, as part of a perfect seven-day Creation week (Genesis 2:2; Exodus 20:8–11).
2. God blessed and sanctified it for the benefit of the human race (Genesis 2:3).

3. God rested on the seventh day from all His work of Creation (Genesis 2:3).
4. The Sabbath is the only day that God calls "My holy day" (Isaiah 58:13).
5. Jesus and His disciples kept the seventh-day Sabbath (cf. Matthew 24:15–17, 20).
6. The persevering saints, just before the second coming, are identified as those "who keep the commandments of God and their faith in Jesus" (Revelation 14:12).
7. The Sabbath is a day of rest, joy, refreshment, healing, and hope.

Seeing that the Sabbath is the only day that offers these benefits, who would even think of observing another day and missing all these blessings?

For further reading:

Andreasen, M. L. *The Sabbath: Which Day and Why?* Takoma Park, Md.: Review and Herald®, 1942.

Bacchiocchi, Samuele. *From Sabbath to Sunday: A Historical Investigation of the Rise of Sunday Observance in Early Christianity.* Rome: Pontifical Gregorian University Press, 1977.

Goldstein, Clifford. *A Pause for Peace: What God's Gift of the Sabbath Can Mean to You.* Boise, Idaho: Pacific Press®, 1992.

Neufeld, Don F., and Julia Neuffer, eds. *Seventh-day Adventist Bible Students' Source Book.* Commentary Reference Series, vol. 9. Washington, D.C.: Review and Herald®, 1962. Sections of special interest: "Sabbath," nos. 1362–1393: 842–863; "Sabbath and Sunday," nos. 1394–1431: 864–883; "Sabbath, Change of," nos. 1431–1456: 883–892; "Sabbath Observance," nos. 1457–1472: 892–898; "Sun Worship," nos. 1567–1579: 965–969; "Sunday," nos. 1580–1641: 969–999; and "Sunday Laws," nos. 1642–1674: 999–1026.

Strand, Kenneth. "The Sabbath." In *Handbook of Seventh-day Adventist Theology*. Edited by Raoul Dederen. Commentary Reference Series, vol. 12. Hagerstown, Md.: Review and Herald®, 2000.

Strand, Kenneth A., ed. *The Sabbath in Scripture and History.* Washington, D.C.: Review and Herald®, 1982.

Werner K. Vyhmeister *was born and educated in Chile at the University of Chile and earned his PhD in 1968. In addition, he completed a BD at Andrews University in 1968. After a few years in pastoral work, he began his teaching and administrative career at Chile Adventist College, then at River Plate Adventist University. For three years (1972–1975), he was director of education for the South American Division. He spent eighteen years at the Adventist Theological Seminary, three of those as associate dean and nine as dean. Between his two Andrews stints, he founded the Adventist International Institute of Advanced Studies (AIIAS) in the Philippines. Since retirement in 2000, he has been a consultant for the General Conference, for the Department of Education, and for the development of the Adventist University of Africa. He and his wife, Nancy, live in Yucaipa, California.*

References

[1] Bible quotations are from the New American Standard Bible.

[2] J. N. Andrews, *History of the Sabbath and the First Day of the Week*, 3rd ed. (Battle Creek, Mich.: Steam Press of the Seventh-day Adventist Publications, 1887), 515, quoted in Ellen G. White, *The Great Controversy* (Mountain View, Calif.: Pacific Press®, 1911), 437.

[3] White, *The Great Controversy*, 438.

LARRY L. LICHTENWALTER

Chapter 12

Are There Moral Absolutes?

"What is truth?" Pilate asked Jesus. A really good question—perhaps the most philosophical question in the entire Bible (John 18:38). This question echoes at the foundation of our secular worldview and culture. Many today are convinced that nothing is absolutely true, that truth may not exist at all, and if it does, it is certainly not self-evident and may not even be knowable. Even more, they say, nothing is completely right or completely wrong. At best there is only a diversity of truths.

This relativistic view of reality and the quality of human experience makes truth "person dependent" or simply "truth for me," relative to one's individual preferences or those of the group to which one belongs. No longer viewed as objective, timeless, or passed down, truth is now created and re-created out of experience, in dialogue with others, and within one's culture. This means that the morals of today are not the morals of yesterday. They are cultural, relative, and shifting according to time and personal or social need or preference. Of course, those who champion the existence of enduring moral, religious, social, or political truth face a barrage of objections about imposing standards on others, intolerance, and oppression. Because moral truth can be deeply polarizing, many find the concept of truth itself dangerous.

Surprisingly, instead of the collapse of morality, this daring relativism has actually spawned a renaissance of searching—often lonely and painful—for principles of life. The angst comes in the perceived pluralism or absence of authority, and the centrality of choice in the self-constitution of postmodern moral agents. The cacophony of moral voices throws the individual back on his or her own subjectivity as the only ultimate ethical authority. The challenge of exploring all possible roads one could travel to know how one should live morally is often soul wearying as well as scary, if not risky.

Pilate never gave Jesus time to answer. Most who ask about truth today don't take the time either. But had he paused long enough to listen, Pilate would have heard some incredible truth about truth—and moral absolutes.

The essence of truth

First, truth exists (John 8:32). Moreover, there is but one way, one truth, and one life (John 14:6). Way, truth, and life are biblical moral expressions. Truth is a moral realm in which one can *stand* and *be* and *act*—even worship (John 3:21; 4:24; 8:44). There is a *spirit of truth* and a *spirit of error,* and no lie is *of* the truth (John 18:27; cf. 1 John 2:21; 4:6). The truth is in contrast to untruth and falsity, unreality and illusion, or any idea of a diversity of truths.

Second, the essence of truth is personal. Before Pilate even asked, Jesus had already declared, "*I am* the way, and the truth, and the life"

(John 14:6; emphasis added).[1] This is a bold biblical delineation: God is truth. His nature, His very spirit, is truth. At its core, truth is a Being.[2] This means truth is both moral and "inherently personal."[3] It is neither abstract nor a mere teaching. It is "first a matter of inner character and only derivatively a quality of words and deeds."[4] All God says and all God does is truth. His words and His works are but revelations of His nature. The teachings of Jesus are true because they express the truth, which He Himself is.[5]

Truth, then, brings us into a personal relationship with the very Source of authentic life. It will always engage us as persons. A truthful Person encounters our person with respect to the truthfulness of our own being and doing. It is a Person who brings example, hope, courage and power to be true in a world of deceit and illusion. This is good news because it makes us something more than mere machines applying correct principles or a code of ethics: it makes us persons. Furthermore, it anchors truth in the supernatural. Truth begins with God, not human beings. Truth is eternal because it resides in God. Truth is unchanging because God does not change. There is a unity of truth because truth comes from the same Source—God. Truth is ultimately God's truth because God is the Source of all truth.

Truth is propositional revelation

Third, God's Word is truth (John 17:17). While the essence of truth is personal, truth can at the same time consist of ideas and words that are concrete, objective, and propositional. Truth as ideas or words can be spoken, heard, written down, read, understood, and kept; it is life transforming. Jesus assumed that truth-filled words and ideas carry understandable form, content, and, most important, meaning. There is correspondence between the ideas and the realities they represent—whether Jesus, His Father, or human moral or spiritual life. Truthful words can be relied on precisely because they both accord with reality and come from the One who is true (John 14:6; cf. Revelation 21:5; 22:6). Because Jesus Himself is both "the Word" and the "truth" such correspondence between words and reality is assured (John 1:1–3, 14; cf. Revelation 19:14; 1 John 1:1).

Truth is the oxygen of the mind. It is the point of departure for all intellectual, spiritual, and moral pursuits and what alone truly frees (John 8:32; Philippians 4:8). We say "true" when we are convinced that reality and our minds match.[6] We say "morally true" when we are convinced that that reality matches our perceptions of what is right, just, and good. Truth is vital, directly influencing our lives. We act upon what we believe to be true, thus shaping the way we live. Truth affects how we see ourselves and view others. Truth is what matters.

Like a navigator who gets bearings from the stars so he can sail at night, we need some fixed points by which we can orient ourselves morally, something outside ourselves. God's Word as truth provides such fixed points for moral orientation. Jesus' statement "Thy Word is truth" (John 17:17) implies revelation, and if revelation is possible, moral absolutes are possible.[7] Moral truth is not constructed, it is revealed; it is discovered and not determined by a majority vote. It is authoritative and not merely a matter of personal preference.

Dostoyevsky's Ivan Karamazov contended that if there is no God, everything is permitted. But if God does exist, then one can expect moral truth to exist as well. And if the absolute standard for morality is God

Himself, every moral action is to be judged in the light of His nature. God's revealed Word—Scripture—is our link both to God and to moral truth. The Bible is our ethical standard because it comes from God, who alone is the standard for morality. This must be kept in mind when we appeal to the Bible in moral matters, for it was written in a different cultural situation and in a different time from our own. "Only the fact that God transcends culture allows us to entertain the hope of using moral principles from the Bible in our [own] culture."[8] Without this we could not hope to rise above cultural relativism. But God is above it. And God has spoken. What God reveals in the Bible applies universally to all cultures.

You can know truth

Fourth, truth can be known: "You will know the truth and the truth will make you free" (John 8:32). Sometimes proof of truth is easily achieved—like at what temperature and altitude water boils or freezes. This is scientific truth, which can usually be objectively verified. Verifying moral truth claims is tougher and more mysterious. Good and evil cannot be directly observed or measured. They require a different approach, but nevertheless can be known with enough certainty to be inwardly orienting. Even our own subjective evaluations of truth can be objective—when we observe cause-and-effect experiences of moral truth lived or not lived in our own lives.

Moral principles correspond to the nature of God and to our own nature as well. Man is not an animal, but a unique moral being.[9] Because we are made in the image of God (Genesis 1:26, 27), we have the capacity to understand what we need to know, both about God and moral life.[10]

When we obey the moral law of God, we are behaving in a manner consistent with the way God made us. Sin or disobedience to the moral law is not only an offense to God, it is a violation of our own created nature.[11] Proverbs puts it succinctly: "He who finds me [God's moral wisdom] finds life . . . but he who sins against me injures himself; all those who hate me love death" (Proverbs 8:35, 36).

Divine revelation means that biblical truth ultimately corresponds to reality as perceived by God, who alone sees reality in all its complexity and fullness. What we understand is partial and limited. There is a difference between the statement that moral absolutes exist and the claim that one can know these absolutes with the same clarity that God knows them. Absolute truth is not the same as absolute knowing. We can only have a relative understanding of absolute truth (1 Corinthians 13:12). Yet partial truth can be real truth, as long as we do not take it for the whole truth. This is inwardly freeing because it gives hope of a fuller understanding even while we live confidently by what we already know (John 7:17).

Truth behaves

Fifth, truth is integrally linked with righteousness (what is upright, good, just, right). Truth is right action. It is ethically correct behavior. Truth encompasses and assumes the moral. It is something that can be expressed in tangible deeds, which in turn reveal the authenticity of one's connection with God, the Source of truth (John 3:21; cf. 5:36; 10:25). Truthful behavior reveals the moral essence of one's very self. It gives witness of the life-changing power of truth (John 17:17). It follows Jesus, whose own works and deeds gave continual witness to the truth itself and to His personal connection with the Father (John 5:36; 10:25, 37; 14:11).

Sixth, truth is relational. It includes speech and transparent behavior before others (John 8:44–46, 55). Truth and the trust it engenders are the foundation of all relationships. No genuine relationship can exist between false selves. Truthfulness cannot be compartmentalized. One cannot be true in one area of life (spiritual, religious, doctrine) and false in another (moral, politics, society, business, marriage) and still be true. Separating the spiritual from the moral divides the person. Subjective selectivity of moral truths divides the person. As Jesus spoke truth (John 8:45, 46) so must we. Just as He exposed the hypocrisy, hidden agendas, and less than transparent ways of Israel's religious leaders, Jesus invites us to a higher level of personal transparency and truthfulness (John 8:44, 55).

Being truthful

Seventh, moral truth will ever be a matter of our own *being*. As with God, the essence of truth on the human level is personal. It concerns our own inner moral consistency. Are we true selves or false selves? Do we love the truth or inwardly seek to evade its claims on our lives? Only those who are "of the truth" (1 John 3:19) will understand and receive truth and, in keeping with the truth, *be truthful* (Revelation 14:5; 22:15; cf. John 18:37). This is the meaning of Jesus' statement: "If anyone is willing to do His will, he will know of the teaching" (John 7:17). The willingness to implement moral truth in one's life and the ability to perceive it are inseparably linked. We know the truth as we live the truth. We reach truth by doing it. "Doing the truth means living out of the reality which is *He* who is the truth, making His being the being of ourselves and of our world."[12]

Are There Moral Absolutes?

Scripture speaks of those who love lies because they do not love truth (2 Thessalonians 2:7–13; cf. John 3:19–21). They believe what is false because they do not love what is true. It becomes a circle. One's inner moral orientation tends either toward truth or falsehood; the practice of either further imprints one's inner world in the respective moral direction.

The real issues regarding the perceived relativity of truth reside here. Many are satisfied that moral truth is relative because it means they can pick and choose their own lives. They don't want moral truths contained in laws to direct their behaviors. This is selfish. If they can relativize truth, then nothing is externally restrictive or binding. Moral truth, then, is not always convenient or valued. Ultimately, as seen with Pilate, the question of truth is also a question about our own selves.

People are rarely across-the-board subjectivists or objectivists. Many who believe in moral absolutes are comfortably relativistic in certain areas, and many who claim to be relativists qualify their relativism. The real issue is not whether truth exists, but where we draw the line that separates matters of fact from issues of opinion or taste. Moral relativism seemingly resonates with our desire to treat people kindly. It offers a way to justify our actions by claiming that ethical standards are personal. It allows for intellectual and character laziness. Defending ideas and moral formation is hard work. Relativism takes the easy way out because it creates the illusion that we don't have to do the heavy lifting of supporting our ideas.[13]

Moral relativism is often reactionary. Christians themselves have been a major cause of moral relativism. Many choose moral relativism over moral absolutes because those who believe in moral absolutes are often fixated on select moral truths (agendas); they appear legalistic, arrogant, unbending, insensitive, abusive, and assert their positions without explanation. We need to admit that we are not God, be humble about ethical issues, listen more carefully to the genuine moral concerns of our times, and think of moral absolutes in terms of character and moral qualities rather than mere actions. Perhaps then there would be less reaction. We should be absolutely just, compassionate, loving, and patient.

Grace-filled truth

Finally, truth and grace go together. They are organically linked, and in no way are they mutually exclusive. The glory of God's character revealed in Jesus was "full of grace and truth" (John 1:14). "Grace and truth were realized through Jesus Christ" (John 1:17). We "[understand] the grace of God in truth" (Colossians 1:6). We are to speak the truth in love (Ephesians 4:15). Grace, mercy, peace, truth, and love are inseparable components of genuine moral and spiritual life (2 John 3). The moral truth of Jesus is never cold or impersonal. It is ever concerned about unique circumstances of real people. It is as gentle as it is forceful. It treats people kindly. Thus, Jesus could at the same time tell the woman caught in adultery, "I do not condemn you, either," and "Go. From now on sin no more" (John 8:11). Jesus, who is "the way, and the truth, and the life," always treated people with understanding, grace, mercy, love—and the truth.

The truth Jesus spoke about incorporates a moral, life-transforming dimension: "You will know the truth, and the truth will make you free." He prayed, "Sanctify them in the truth; Your word is truth" (John 8:32; 17:17). "We do not so much need freedom in order to discover truth, as we are to reside in truth in order to experience freedom."[14]

Are there moral absolutes? Of course! As an infinite, eternal pattern, truth lies at the heart of the Christian worldview. We are to seek it, believe it, live it, model it, and speak it. We must make decisions based on it and be transformed by it. A battle for moral truth lies at the heart of the great controversy between Christ and Satan. It is a battle for our minds and characters as we live life and are engaged in the final showdown of earth's history (2 Thessalonians 2:8–12; Revelation 12:17; 14:6–13; 16:12–16). God has given His Spirit to guide us toward truth (John 16:13). At every step, Jesus would remind us, "I am the way, and the truth, and the life."

For further reading:
Explore the books and articles that appear in the citations.

Larry L. Lichtenwalter holds a PhD in Christian ethics and has been lead pastor of the Village Seventh-day Adventist Church in Berrien Springs, Michigan, since 1985. With the Adventist Theological Society, he is involved in theological nurture on an international level. He is writing a book on the moral themes of the Apocalypse, and teaches Principles of Christian Ethics, Preaching From Revelation, and other courses at Andrews University Theological Seminary. He has written several books, the latest of which is Revelation's Great Love Story *(2008)*. He has published more than thirty articles in various Adventist periodicals. He and his wife, Kathie, have five sons.

References

[1] All biblical references in this chapter are quoted from the New American Standard Bible.

[2] John Wesley Taylor, "Is Truth of Consequence?," *Perspective Digest* 14, no. 3 (2009): 9.

[3] Arthur F. Holmes, *All Truth Is God's Truth* (Downers Grove, Ill.: InterVarsity, 1983), 34.

[4] Ibid.

⁵ Paul Tillich, "What Is Truth," *Canadian Journal of Theology* 1, no. 2 (1955): 120.

⁶ Daniel C. Maguire, *Ethics: A Complete Method for Moral Choice* (Minneapolis, Minn.: Fortress, 2010), 15.

⁷ Erwin W. Lutzer, *The Necessity of Ethical Absolutes* (Grand Rapids, Mich.: Zondervan, 1981), 70.

⁸ Ibid.

⁹ Human beings possess (1) the capacity for self-reflection; (2) the ability to reason; (3) moral capacity, i.e., we can understand distinctions between good and evil; and (4) the capacity to be rightly related to God.

¹⁰ Art Lindsley, *True Truth: Defending Absolute Truth in A Relativistic World* (Downers Grove, Ill.: InterVarsity, 2004), 19.

¹¹ Lutzer, *The Necessity of Ethical Absolutes*, 70.

¹² Tillich, "What Is Truth," 121.

¹³ Steve Wilkens, *Hidden Worldviews: Eight Cultural Stories That Shape Our Lives* (Downers Grove, Ill.: InterVarsity, 2009), 86.

¹⁴ Taylor, "Is Truth of Consequence?" 23.

STEPHEN BAUER

Chapter 13

If God Is Good and All-powerful, How Can He Allow Suffering?

As a father, I have vivid and poignant memories of taking my three-year-old son for hernia surgery. He clung to his mother like a leech, clearly distressed and afraid of the medical personnel who came to prepare him for the surgery. From his childish perspective, he must have wondered why Mommy and Daddy, who had always sought to protect his comfort, now allowed strangers to poke, prod, and otherwise make him uncomfortable. The Mommy and Daddy he knew to that point had protected him from such painful indignities, but now seemed to have turned against him. Why?

Just as my little son must have questioned his parents' wisdom, so we are tempted to question how a good yet all-powerful God permits suffering. This problem has vexed thinkers for millennia. Attempts to reconcile a world of suffering with a good yet all-powerful God are called *theodicy,* quite literally the justification of God. The full statement of the problem theodicy seeks to solve can be stated this way: if God is good and loving yet also all-powerful, why does He allow such suffering?

Peter Bertocci lists four standard Christian responses to the problem of evil. First, God did not will evil but allowed it in order to give true freedom to man. Second, suffering is part of God's ultimate plan for achieving some overall greater good. Third, natural evil is a tool God uses to achieve the best possible world. Finally, in what seems a variant of the third option, suffering prepares man for a joyous eternity with God. It is a disciplinary tool for man's refinement and purification in preparation for eternal life.[1]

It can easily be seen that all four traditional forms of Christian responses may well overlap and interact with each other. Certainly, it appears that all four of these emphases can be found to some degree in Ellen White's writings. She ascribes our freedom of choice to being part of God's master plan to permit true freedom for created moral agents. For example, "For the good of the entire universe through ceaseless ages Satan must more fully develop his [Satan's] principles, that his charges against the divine government might be seen in their true light by all created beings, and that the justice and mercy of God and the immutability of His law might forever be placed beyond all question."[2] Again she asserts,

> God might have created man without the power to transgress His law; He might have withheld the hand of Adam from touching the forbidden fruit; but in that case man would have been, not a free moral agent, but a mere automaton. Without freedom of choice, his obedience would not have been voluntary, but forced. There could have been no development of character. Such a course would have been contrary to God's plan in dealing with the inhabitants of other worlds. It would have been unworthy of man as an intelligent being, and would have sustained Satan's charge of God's arbitrary rule.[3]

If God Is Good and All-powerful, How Can He Allow Suffering?

Thus, White would seem to be partly aligned with the freedom theory, and partly in the genre of work that explains natural evil in terms of being permitted for a greater long-term good. This mixture of the freedom and greater-good arguments seems to suggest the conclusion that Ellen White's great controversy model is a form of the best-possible-world genre of theodicy. In her view, to get the best possible world, God takes some risks involving freedom and character development, risking a temporary season of natural evil as part of achieving that goal.

Certainly, the great controversy helps to explain the presence of evil around us, and can give an individual who is suffering a sense of personal significance as a contributor to a grand cosmic cause. But the great controversy still leaves the question of why God chose to permit this kind of freedom, with the ensuing consequences, especially when He has the power to terminate the problem. Participation in a cosmic cause may bring some meaning and comfort, but, like Job's three friends, may not be the most effective comforter in encounters with natural evil.

I do not propose to definitively solve the problem of theodicy. Rather, I shall offer a personal, perhaps unique, perspective on the problem. It comes not from theologians or philosophers, but from my wrestling, *sola Scriptura,* during the process of my mother's untimely death due to cancer, with the problem of why good people suffer. Bertocci would, no doubt, classify it as a mix of the greater good and disciplinary genres.

Theological basis

So why then might a good and powerful God permit suffering? Our quest begins in Genesis 1–3.[4] God created Adam and Eve and placed them in the Garden of Eden. Humans were not left absolutely free to do or to be whatever they wanted. Rather, in creating human beings, God exercised His right to create with specific intentions, boundaries, limitations, and purposes. Thus, they were not allowed to eat whatever they wanted. The fruit of one tree was off-limits. Furthermore, lest their labors so absorb them that they would forget who they were in relation to God, the Sabbath rest was instituted to remind them of who God is and who they were—finite creatures under the sovereignty of an infinite God. These two aspects of the Creation order seem especially designed to help Adam and Eve recognize their places as creatures under the sovereignty of a Creator—creatures with the inherent limitations that characterize finite, created beings.

The temptation scene at the forbidden tree highlights the issue of recognizing one's own limitations as a creature. The snake is introduced as the craftiest creature God made (Genesis 3:1). Snakes are not known for possessing powers of human language and reason. How, then, did the snake suddenly acquire the ability to talk and reason? By all appearances, the snake had transcended his divinely determined design limitations by eating the forbidden fruit.[5] The snake's fundamental temptation, then, was that just as he had transcended his God-given limits by eating the forbidden fruit, Eve could do so as well and become "like God." She thought to become a co-deity in a collegial divine relationship instead of remaining a creature under divine sovereignty.

The apparent success of the snake in transcending his creation limits would seem to be a highly compelling and formidable temptation. The forcefulness of this temptation was further multiplied by the fact that when Eve assessed the tree, it looked "pleasing to the eyes" and appeared to be "good for food." By contrast, God had said that the tree was dangerous—you eat, you die—but the tree looked anything but dangerous.

The tree thus appeared to be a way to transcend her finite limits and become elevated to a parity with God. It seems to me, then, that the fall of Eve was precisely rooted in a rejection of God's design parameters, with their accompanying limitations, and a desire to transcend them and cast them off. Adam's eating of the fruit signified his choice to join Eve in the same quest. Mankind's fall came through a failure to accept their God-given limitations and acknowledge who they were as perfect but limited creatures under the sovereign authority of their Creator.

The purpose of natural evil

How can a good God address the problem? God first conducted an investigative judgment to call Adam and Eve to accountability for how they used their free will. If God merely winked at the situation, He would make Himself a liar, having threatened consequences—dying that day—without delivering. Such a move would undermine His sovereignty, for His word would not be reliable. But man was deceived. Could humans be corrected to acknowledge again their proper position under a Creator? How then did God go about correcting humans who had refused to acknowledge their limitations and His sovereignty?

The answer is simple. The judgments pronounced in Genesis 3—painful childbirth, subservice of wife to husband, thorns, thistles, cursed ground, sweaty brows, and finally death—share one common denominator: They all express an increase of finite limitations on Adam and Eve. The intensity of the limitation is increased in an effort to get Adam and Eve, along with us, to properly acknowledge our place under God's sovereignty. Death becomes the ultimate limitation, a barrier we are unable to transcend.

A final limitation of human beings is that they not only lost their sovereignty over the earth, but now found themselves under the sovereignty of a hostile power—sin. Satan became the "god of this world" (2 Corinthians 4:4) and the dual powers of sin and death reigned supreme (Romans 5:12–21). Adam and Eve could not bequeath to their children what they no longer possessed. As subjects of sin and death, their children were born subject to the same powers, in need of a Deliverer. All are under sin as a reigning power (Romans 3:9). Slaves give birth to slaves, not to freemen, and every individual is "sold under sin" (Romans 7:14). In Romans 7, the slave of sin can see and appreciate what is good, but is not free to do it. Even his will is limited. Enslavement to sin is the ultimate demonstration of our limits as creatures under God, demonstrating our need of a Deliverer to tame that power for us (Romans 7:24, 25). Natural evil thus ultimately shows us whose power we and the world are under, and calls us to acknowledge our limits and depend on a God who is wiser than we are and sovereign over us. What then, does it mean to acknowledge our limits before God?

Finding meaning in suffering

The first part of acknowledging our limits as creatures is to acknowledge mystery. Just as my son at the age of three did not have the frame of reference to adequately understand why Mommy and Daddy allowed strangers to inflict pain and suffering on him in a hospital, so we do not have the cosmic contextual data or the capacity of wisdom to understand why God permits many things. As rational thinking adults, we do not like to admit there are mysteries we cannot decipher. Job provides a classic case study of this confrontation with mystery beyond human comprehension. Job is never informed about the cosmic argument between God and Satan that led to his suffering, and thus he had no frame of reference to adequately understand his situation. Instead, he had to acknowledge his limitations by submitting to the mystery and continuing to trust and serve God faithfully.

Part of the problem of evil is our stubborn refusal to acknowledge our limited perspective and wisdom. Modern humans are highly educated and have accomplished much in transcending some of the limits of the curse of sin through technological prowess. Hence, with our great accomplishments in fighting against our limits, we become overly optimistic in our abilities to decipher and understand everything. Thus, genuine mysteries, such as the problem of evil, vex us when we cannot satisfactorily explain them.

The problem of evil should help us acknowledge our limitations and accept that there are mysteries beyond our capacities to understand and interpret, and that God may well be accomplishing a greater good that we cannot understand. These limitations are a call to us to renounce our rejection of God's designs and purposes for us as His creatures, and reveal our need of His sustenance and governance. Natural evil should thus be seen as a tool to help teach us our limits and our need of God, partly imposed by God and partly caused by Satan's usurping of dominion over this world and wreaking havoc as he tries to transcend his own God-given limits.[6]

A final limitation imposed on us is that God has delivered humans over to the fruits of their choices (Romans 1:18–28) to help us bottom out and call on Him. To shield us from this confrontation with the results of our choices would enable our soul-destroying revolt against God's design limits, harming our eternal destiny without challenge. Such a protection from our choices would thus be patently unloving. "Those whom I love,

I reprove and chasten; so be zealous and repent" (Revelation 3:19). We, however, have a difficult time seeing this approach as loving, precisely due to our limitations, especially death. How then, can we believe it is loving for God to permit undeserved death such as in an earthquake, flood, or even at the hands of man?

God's larger perspective

We must remember that God is not limited by death as we are. We feel great pressure to solve issues in our lifetimes. Resurrection allows issues to be addressed and solved in ways not available when limited by death. Natural evil is problematic to us, in part because of our mortality. Undeserved death, whether by natural disaster or the agency of evil persons, makes us reckon with the problems of eternity, confronts us with our lack of Godlike power to sustain our own safety, and thus helps us to acknowledge who we are as limited creatures in need of God.

The use of suffering and adversity as a disciplinary tool begs the question, Does God use immoral means to accomplish moral ends? Since the apostle Paul rejects doing evil to produce good results (Romans 3:8), it would seem problematic for God to practice what He inspired Paul to condemn. It is precisely God's lack of limitation in reference to our dying that frees Him from such accusations.

Let me illustrate from my experience as a flight instructor. As the instructor, I would sometimes allow students to exceed their limitations in order to learn important lessons, but I would not allow the situation to get so out of control that it endangered the student's welfare (or my own!). Some things I could not allow, as I would have no power to recover the situation. By contrast, while God will not let a situation endanger our eternal welfare against our will, He may allow suffering and even death to confront us and push us towards corrections compatible with eternal life, for He has the power to recover us from all of that and more. If He did not have those powers, then, and only then, could we charge Him with using immoral means to accomplish moral ends. Rather, He makes use of the imposition of greater limits and Satan's volitional activity as disciplinary tools to help us bottom out so we will look up to Him and be saved eternally.[7]

I was forcibly made to wrestle with these concepts during the process of my mother's death. As she slowly passed away, I was thoroughly confronted with my limitations as a creature in a sinful world. I felt powerless, wishing I could save my mom and not being able to do so. Philosophical nuances seem irrelevant at such times, too easily leading to greater questioning of God than deeper trust in Him. But the hope of resurrection allowed me to see her death as confronting her family, friends, and acquaintances with their limitations, their need of Someone bigger and wiser than themselves, and to accept my limitations, which like my son, God may allow my mother, myself, and my family to suffer for greater good that we cannot now understand.

The fundamental message of the fledgling church was very simple: Jesus Christ has the solution to death. Man has tried and continues to try to solve the riddle of death through better technology. We have had some success in forestalling death, but cannot conquer it. In the end, death forces us to admit that we are limited creatures in need of a Life-Giver who can conquer the powers of sin and death. When we acknowledge who God is, and receive by faith the deliverance secured for us by Christ, then natural evil will have achieved the purpose God designs for it, namely the surrender necessary for our eternal salvation.

For further reading:

Lewis, C. S. *The Problem of Pain: How Human Suffering Raises Almost Intolerable Intellectual Problems.* New York: Macmillan, 1962.

Draper, Paul. "Pain and Pleasure: An Evidential Problem for Theists." *Nous* 23 (1989): 341. Republished in *The Evidential Argument From Evil.* Edited by Daniel Howard-Snyder, 12–29. Indianapolis, Ind.: Indiana University Press, 1996.

Plantinga, Alvin. "Epistemic Probability and Evil." In *The Evidential Argument From Evil.* Edited by Daniel Howard-Snyder. Indianapolis, Ind.: Indiana University Press, 1996.

Stackhouse, John G., Jr. *Can God Be Trusted? Faith and the Challenge of Evil.* Downers Grove, Ill.: InterVarsity Press, 2009.

White, Ellen G. "The Origin of Evil." In *The Great Controversy,* 492–504. Washington, D.C.: Review and Herald®, 1911.

———. "Why Was Sin Permitted?" In *Patriarchs and Prophets,* 33–43. Mountain View, Calif.: Pacific Press®, 1913.

———. "Bible Biographies." In *Education,* 155–158. Mountain View, Calif.: Pacific Press®, 1952.

Wright, N. T. *Evil and the Justice of God.* Downers Grove, Ill.: InterVarsity Press, 2006.

Stephen Bauer *is a professor of religion at Southern Adventist University, where he has been teaching since 1999. He completed a PhD in religion at Andrews University in 2006, with a concentration in systematic theology and ethics. He served as a district pastor from 1983 to 1989 in the Greater New York Conference, and from 1997 to 1999 in the Southern New England Conference. While taking doctoral classes at Andrews University, he became a certified flight instructor. His teaching is mostly in the area of systematic theology and ethics; he also guides*

If God Is Good and All-powerful, How Can He Allow Suffering?

students through the maze of biblical Hebrew. He was the first professor in the School of Religion to develop and maintain a Web site for his students. He is active in academic societies and currently is president of the Adventist Theological Society. A highlight of his teaching career was a two-week class on salvation that he taught in China. His favorite topic of study, teaching, and preaching is how God delivers from the power of sin and transforms lives.

References

[1] Peter Bertocci, *Introduction to the Philosophy of Religion* (New York: Prentice Hall, 1951), 401–408.

[2] See Ellen G. White, *The Great Controversy* (Washington, D.C.: Review and Herald®, 1911), 497, where she has strong overtones of the freedom argument followed by the greater good/best possible world aspect on page 498. See also, White, *Testimonies for the Church* (Mountain View, Calif.: Pacific Press®, 1948), 3:115. White presents an example of interpreting suffering as a means of divine discipline.

[3] White, *Patriarchs and Prophets* (Washington, D.C.: Review and Herald®, 1958), 49. See also, White, *The Great Controversy* (Mountain View, Calif.: Pacific Press®, 1950), 492–504, 662–678.

[4] Bible quotations are from the Revised Standard Version.

[5] This inference is clearly asserted by Ellen G. White. See White, *The Story of Redemption* (Washington, D.C.: Review and Herald®, 1947), 34.

[6] The idea that suffering is a tool to help us recognize our weakness and need of God is echoed in Paul's second letter to the Corinthians. Paul describes his experience with the metaphor of having an unwanted "thorn . . . in the flesh" (2 Corinthians 12:7–10). The nature of this "thorn" is not explicitly stated in the text. It is not clear whether this "thorn" was a natural evil, yet it is quite possible that it was. Paul reminds the Galatians how they would have exchanged their eyes for his if they could have (Galatians 4:15), suggesting Paul had some kind of chronic eye problem associated with a natural evil scenario. Since it is quite possible this "thorn" was some kind of natural evil that Paul could not escape, how Paul interprets that thorn and invests it with meaning seems instructive to us in how we can deal with the problem of evil. Paul here seems to depict uncontrollable suffering—both from natural and moral evils—as a tool to teach him the unboastful dependence on God necessary for a healthy spiritual life. Paul uses this same theology of limitations in arguing for applying church discipline. Two times (1 Corinthians 5:5; 1 Timothy 1:20) Paul makes a curious statement about delivering someone to Satan for corrective-disciplinary purposes.

[7] The use of natural suffering for disciplinary measures is applied to the incarnate Christ. "For it was fitting that he, for whom and by whom all things exist, in bringing many sons to glory, should make the pioneer of their salvation perfect through suffering" (Hebrews 2:10; cf. 5:8, 9). Christ, as a Man, had to practice the art of acknowledging limitations and submitting to God's designs and purposes for Him. Hence He was subject to hunger, thirst, accidents, and bereavement as we are, and also to real temptation. His acceptance of God's purposes, and their accompanying limitations is most poignantly expressed in His prayer in Gethsemane, "Not as I will, but as thou wilt" (Matthew 26:39 ; cf. 26:42; Luke 22:42).

EKKEHARDT MUELLER

Chapter 14

What Happens to Us After We Die?

The question of what happens after death haunts many, who try to avoid thinking about death or an afterlife. The issue has confronted humanity since its earliest days. All cultures and world religions have tried to find out what happens after death. The Egyptians developed an extensive mummification process and built pyramids as tombs for the greatest among them. The Greeks got involved in philosophical speculations. In Plato's *Phaedo,* Socrates tries to prove the immortality of the soul through logical reasoning.[1] Some Eastern religions have opted for the concept of reincarnation.[2]

"Is death necessary?" asked biologist G. R. Taylor, as he discussed research on the problem of aging and dying and the possibility of bringing about natural immortality through scientific advances.[3] In the meantime, some have decided to be frozen, to be revived when cures for their diseases or the aging process has been found. Many others—especially Christians—follow Greek speculation and claim that although their bodies are mortal, their souls are not. Most humans seem to hope that death is not the end.

From the problem toward a solution

Unlike animals, humans have the unique ability to reflect on their own deaths. However, while we live with the awareness that our lives are limited, we have a hard time imagining what it means to be gone forever. Yet we also have a hard time thinking that we could live forever.

The problem is that our deceased loved ones do not and obviously cannot inform us about life after death (Luke 16:27–29). There are so-called near-death experiences, but even then, people may be able to relate only how they experienced the dying process from which they recovered. In addition, these experiences can be interpreted differently.[4] There are also spiritualistic phenomena, in which supposed spirits of the deceased appear, but they are oftentimes scary and vague and provide no real proof of life after death. From a biblical standpoint, they could either be illusions or the appearance of demonic spirits since even Satan "disguises himself as an angel of light" (2 Corinthians 11:14, NASB).

Obituaries and inscriptions on gravestones claim that God has taken loved ones to a better world; others reflect no hope. The obituary in 1 Corinthians 15:3–8 contains four statements that help us to find an approach to our query: (1) Christ has died; (2) Christ was buried; (3) Christ rose from the dead; and (4) Christ appeared to different persons. Jesus Christ came back from the dead, and He knows exactly what is going on when humans die. He has experienced death Himself, and through Scripture, He gives us important information about this topic.

A biblical doctrine of death and afterlife should accommodate all the evidence of the Word of God, creating a unified picture in which clear and difficult texts are well integrated. To learn from Scripture, Christians should "listen with complete objectivity to what the texts teach us about the faith and hope of primitive Christianity, without mixing their own opinions and views that are so dear to them with the interpretation of the texts."[5]

Death in Scripture

The cause of death

According to Genesis 2:17, God announced that death would become a reality if our first parents decided against the Creator. At that time, death and its consequences were foreign to planet Earth. However, the serpent—identified as Satan in Revelation 12:9—claimed that immortality is part of humanity (Genesis 3:4). From the beginning, God's statement about death and Satan's statement about immortality are diametrically opposed. After the Fall (Genesis 3), when the possibility of death became a bitter reality, affecting all human beings (Romans 6:23) and even nonhuman existence (Romans 8:20–22), Satan's lie lived on in the concept of the immortality of the soul. While God was undeniably right that death had come as a consequence of separation from Him, some claimed that a part of human existence was immortal. This characteristic of paganism, not found in Old Testament religion, crept into Judaism in the intertestamental period; from there, it came into Christianity.

The state of the dead

Death in the Old Testament. In order to understand death, it is helpful to return to Creation, because, in some respects, death is an undoing of creation. Genesis 2:7 reports that God gave life to the human body He had shaped from the dust of the ground. The process can be described as dust receiving the spark of life or, biblically speaking, "the breath of life," and thus becoming a living being. As soon as life is withdrawn, the former state—dust—reappears. This applies to humans as well as to animals (cf. Ecclesiastes 3:19, 20). Therefore, it is obvious that in death there is no activity (Ecclesiastes 9:5, 6, 10). The deceased have no consciousness. Already in the Old Testament, death is compared to sleep (Daniel 12:2, 13), which implies unconsciousness: the dead are "sleeping" or "resting" in the earth. However, there will be an awakening or resurrection.[6]

Death in the New Testament. The New Testament confirms that the dead are in the grave (John 5:28, 29). David, a man after God's heart (Acts 13:22), rests in the tomb and is not yet with God (Acts 2:29, 34). Jesus informs His disciples that where He will be, they cannot come immediately (John 7:33, 34; 13:33). They will not have access to the heavenly glory by following Him in death. "Peter is told that though he cannot follow Jesus now, one day he will (verse 36); the whole disciple group is assured that the departure of Jesus has in view the goal of their being with him in the Father's house forever (14:2, 3)."[7] The imagery of sleep is used to describe death. For instance, Lazarus sleeps in death for four days before he is raised by Jesus (John 11:11–15, 17; see also Matthew 27:52; 1 Corinthians 15:6, 18, 20; 1 Thessalonians 4:13–15).[8] The Old and New Testaments, as well as Jesus' own experience, suggest that death is a state of unconsciousness, called sleep.

After death

However, death is not the end. There will be a resurrection (1 Corinthians 15:42–44). Believers will receive new bodies, not unrelated to our present bodies. While we have no detailed information regarding these new bodies, someone has compared our present bodies to coal and the new bodies to a marvelous diamond. Both consist of carbon, and yet they are different from each other. A child of God expects the resurrection (1 Corinthians 15:22, 23). Furthermore, Jesus said He was preparing dwelling places for His people to inhabit after His second coming (John 14:1–3). Finally, death will be done away with (Revelation 21:4).

The immortal soul and Scripture

Scripture and immortality

Only two biblical passages use the word *immortality* (*athanasia*), literally "deathlessness." In 1 Timothy 6:14–16, Paul clearly states that God alone possesses immortality. In 1 Corinthians 15:53, immortality is something humans acquire only at the Second Coming. Believers who have passed away will be resurrected and believers who are alive at Jesus' return will be transformed and receive new and immortal bodies. Therefore, the claim that "immortality is a gift to all men in virtue of their creation and it is the total man which is immortal"[9] is farfetched. The New Testament stresses that eternal life is always dependent on Jesus. Without a saving relationship with Him, there is no everlasting life, not on earth, or in heaven, and certainly not in hell (Romans 6:23; John 3:36; 5:24; 1 John 5:11, 12). "The fate of the unredeemed is not immortality in hell, but the denial to them of immortality."[10]

Another word, *aphtharsia,* describes what is imperishable and incorruptible. The very same results appear: God, divine qualities, and the inheritance He offers are incorruptible (e.g., Romans 1:23; 1 Timothy 1:17; 1 Peter 1:4, 23; 3:4). Incorruptibility is a future gift to be received by believers at the resurrection (1 Corinthians 15:42, 50, 52–54). Thus, it can be safely affirmed that immortality is not inherent in human beings.[11]

Scripture and the soul

The Hebrew and Greek terms that are translated as "soul" can be rendered in different ways. They stand for "life" (Genesis 9:4; Matthew 2:20, NASB), "heart" ("doing the will of God from the heart" [Ephesians 6:6, NASB]), emotions (the soul loves or grieves [Song of Solomon 1:7; Mark 14:34]), and frequently for the entire person, as the following instances show: (1) humans do not have a soul but are a soul (1 Corinthians 15:45; Genesis 2:7); (2) even animals are souls, that is, living beings (Genesis 1:20; 9:10; Revelation 16:3); (3) the soul can weep (Jeremiah 13:17); (4) the soul can be taken captive (Jeremiah 52:28–30); (5) the soul can be baptized (Acts 2:41); and quite important (6) the soul can die (Ezekiel 18:4; James 5:20; Revelation 20:4; Psalm 89:48; Job 36:14; Leviticus 19:8; 21:1, 11). From that perspective it is difficult to understand that M. E. Osterhaven, after providing a correct definition of soul, can write that in Scripture the soul "is conceived to be an immaterial principle created by God, which is usually united to a body and gives it life, however, the soul continues to exist after death in human beings."[12] Although he provides some biblical texts, most are the ones listed above that indicate directly or indirectly that the soul may die.

Quite often the term *soul* designates the entire human being: the soul that weeps is the person who weeps. Where soul is distinguished from body, it does not describe a part that can be separated and live independently. Furthermore, the term is not used in connection with immortality. "Neither *nephesh* [the Hebrew term for "soul"] nor *psychē* [the Greek term for "soul"] connotes an immaterial, immortal entity or part of humanity, capable of independent, conscious existence apart from the body."[13]

Consequences

The acceptance of the unbiblical concept of the immortality of the soul has led to a number of serious consequences, to erroneous doctrines and practices, and to distortions of the biblical message.

Other unbiblical teachings and practices. Unbiblical doctrines and practices derived from the immortality concept include (1) a presently burning purgatory and/or hell; (2) indulgences; (3) prayers, alms, and masses for the dead; (4) the veneration of Mary and the saints (cf. 1 Timothy 2:5; Exodus 20:4); (5) the teaching of reincarnation; and (6) the practice of spiritualism (Deuteronomy 18:10–12; 2 Corinthians 11; 14).

Biblical teachings are obscured. Through the centuries, the second coming of Jesus lost its importance in many churches. With the decline of the hope of the Second Coming, the teaching of the resurrection of the dead was partially lost. Also the teaching of the judgment at the end of the world's history became superfluous, since souls were believed to be already in heaven, purgatory, or hell.

God's character is darkened. If the concept of natural immortality were true, God would be a liar who cannot be trusted (cf. Genesis 2:17). God would also be without compassion, allowing people in heaven to watch the pain and suffering of their loved ones still on earth. God would be an unjust tyrant who punishes people in hell forever, when they have sinned for a limited time. The doctrine of the natural immortality of the soul creates a cruel picture of God and distorts Scripture, which teaches that God is love and cares for us (1 John 4:8, 9; Malachi 1:2).

We have to make a decision whom to trust.

God's Statement	_Satan's Statement_
You will surely die.	You surely will not die.
Jesus is the gate to eternal life.	Death is the gate to eternal life.

Difficult passages

A number of passages appear to conflict with what has been said. A careful study of these creates an integrated biblical doctrine. Two will be considered.

The parable of the rich man and Lazarus. Luke 16:19–31 records Jesus' parable of the rich man and Lazarus. After his death, poor Lazarus is carried to Abraham's bosom, while the rich man is tormented in a place separated by a chasm from the place of bliss. Yet Lazarus is able to talk to Abraham, who is within seeing distance, a concept irreconcilable with the biblical teaching of the new earth. It is often held that this parable teaches the immortality of the soul and a kind of already existing hell. The context and the passage itself indicate that Jesus' message was not about the state of the dead but about how to live and the need for accepting Scripture: "They have Moses and the Prophets; let them hear them. . . . If they do not listen to Moses and the Prophets, they will not be persuaded even if someone rises from the dead" (Luke 16:29, 31, NASB). Jesus simply used a well-known story to illustrate important truths, without endorsing the story. In parables, details should not be interpreted unless Scripture does it. An Old Testament illustration for this truth is found in Judges 9:8–16, where trees talk and elect a king. Here the punch line is that the one who was most unworthy has usurped the kingship. Careful scholars do not base biblical doctrines on parables or similes because these are often figurative (as the trees clapping in Isaiah 55:12).

Access to Paradise. Since the old manuscripts were uncials (written with capital letters only) with no punctuation and no space between the words, Luke 23:43 can be translated, "Truly I say to you, today you shall be with Me in Paradise" (NASB), or "Truly I say to you today, you shall be with me in Paradise." According to John 20:17, on Sunday, Jesus had not yet ascended to His Father. He was not in Paradise on Friday, but rested in the grave. Thus, the second translation option is preferable.

Conclusion

While Seventh-day Adventists are in the minority of Christian groups holding this view of what happens after death, several Protestant scholars have affirmed conditional immortality, the sleep of death, and the resurrection. Among these are Oscar Cullman, Emil Brunner, Reinhold Niebuhr, and more recently, J. W. Wenham, J. R. Stott, and Clark H. Pinnock.[14]

Since death reaches out to all human beings, we must prepare for it (Psalm 90:12) by setting our priorities straight. In ancient Thessalonica, two burial inscriptions were found, obviously from the same period. One says, "No hope." The other one reads, "Christ is my life." Two inscriptions and two different philosophies of life: resignation and assurance. What about your life?

For further reading:

Andreasen, Niels-Erik. "Death: Origin, Nature and Final Eradication." In *Handbook of Seventh-day Adventist Theology.* Edited by Raoul Dederen, 314–346. Hagerstown, Md.: Review and Herald®, 2000.

Bacchiocchi, Samuele. *Immortality or Resurrection? A Biblical Study on Human Nature and Destiny.* Berrien Springs, Mich.: Biblical Perspectives, 1997.

Mueller, Ekkehardt. "Punishment of the Wicked." Biblical Research Institute. http://www.adventistbiblicalresearch.org/Biblequestions/punishment.htm.

———. "Watch Out for Hell." Biblical Research Institute. http://www.adventistbiblicalresearch.org/Bible%20Study/Watch%20Out%20for%20Hell.pdf.

Rodriguez, Angel Manuel. "Body Check." Biblical Research Institute. http://www.adventistbiblicalresearch.org/Biblequestions/bodycheck.htm.

———. "From Life to Life." Biblical Research Institute. http://www.adventistbiblicalresearch.org/Biblequestions/fromlifetolife.htm.

———. "Soul Talk." Biblical Research Institute. http://www.adventistbiblicalresearch.org/Biblequestions/soultalk.htm.

———. "What Tales Do the Dead Tell?" Biblical Research Institute. http://www.adventistbiblicalresearch.org/Biblequestions/talesdeadtell.htm.

Seventh-day Adventists Believe: A Biblical Exposition of Fundamental Doctrines. 2nd ed. Silver Spring, Md.: Ministerial Association of the General Conference, 2005.

Ekkehardt Mueller, *a native of Germany, has a ThD and DMin from Andrews University, showing his interest in both theory and practice. He served as a pastor in Bavaria, Germany, from 1972 to 1993. Then he became education director and ministerial secretary of the South German Union. In 1995, he became ministerial secretary of the Euro-Africa Division. For more than a decade, he has been working at the Biblical Research Institute of the General Conference of Seventh-day Adventists, where he now serves as the deputy director. He has written several books and more than two hundred articles. Inheritance seems to work: one of his sons is currently studying for his ThD; the other works for the Southeastern California Conference. His wife teaches at Washington Adventist University.*

Always Prepared

References

[1] See "Phaedo," Wikipedia, accessed March 4, 2010, http://en.wikipedia.org/wiki/Phaedo.

[2] E.g., Malcolm David Eckel, *Buddhism* (New York: Oxford University Press, 2002), 87–95; "Reincarnation," Wikipedia, accessed March 4, 2010, http://en.wikipedia.org/wiki/Reincarnation_and_Hinduism.

[3] Gordon Rattray Taylor, *Die biologische Zeitbombe: Revolution der modernen Biologie* (Frankfurt: Fischer Taschenbuch Verlag, 1971), 11, 12, 95–130.

[4] One of the first researchers in this area was the Swiss-born Elisabeth Kübler-Ross, a psychiatrist. She published numerous books, first about the dying process and later near-death experiences. She became interested in spiritualism and attempted to contact the dead (see "Elisabeth Kübler-Ross," Wikipedia, http://en.wikipedia.org/wiki/Elisabeth_K%C3%BCbler-Ross).

[5] Oscar Cullmann, *Immortality of the Soul or Resurrection of the Dead?* (New York: Macmillan, 1958), 6. Cullmann rejects the doctrine of the immortality of the soul as a Greek belief.

[6] Harrison describes what he calls "soul sleep" but is opposed to it, claiming the word *sleep* "is intended to apply to the body," thereby obviously dividing the body from the soul. "Body" is also used for the entire person, e.g., Rev. 18:14. E. F. Harrison, "Soul Sleep," *Evangelical Dictionary of Theology*, ed. Walter A. Elwell (Grand Rapids, Mich.: Baker Book House, 1984), 1037, 1038.

[7] George R. Beasley-Murray, *John*, Word Biblical Commentary, vol. 36 (Dallas: Word, 2002), 246.

[8] "The revelation to Martha [John 11:25, 26] is thus an assurance of resurrection to the kingdom of God in its consummation through him who is the Resurrection, and of life in the kingdom of God in the present time through him who is the Life." Ibid., 191.

[9] A. F. Johnson, "Conditional Immortality," *Evangelical Dictionary of Theology*, 261.

[10] *Seventh-day Adventist Bible Dictionary* (Washington, D.C.: Review and Herald®, 1960), s.v. "Immortality." See also Ekkehardt Mueller, "Watch Out for Hell," Biblical Research Institute, http://www.adventistbiblicalresearch.org/Bible%20Study/Watch%20Out%20for%20Hell.pdf.

[11] Cf. D. W. Kerr, "Immortality," in *Evangelical Dictionary of Theology*, 551, 552. Kerr makes a number of correct statements, but based on 2 Corinthians 5:8 concludes that "believers who have died are present with the Lord when they are absent from the body," which would be prior to resurrection. However, for a discussion of the text, see Angel Manuel Rodriguez, "From Life to Life," Biblical Research Institute, http://www.adventistbiblicalresearch.org/Biblequestions/fromlifetolife.htm.

[12] M. E. Osterhaven, "Soul," in *Evangelical Dictionary of Theology*, 1037.

[13] *Seventh-day Adventist Encyclopedia,* 2nd rev. ed. (Hagerstown, Md.: Review and Herald®, 1996), 2:629, s.v. "Soul."

[14] Aecio Cairus, "The Doctrine of Man," in *Handbook of SDA Theology*, ed. Raoul Dederen, Commentary Reference Series, vol. 12 (Hagerstown, Md.: Review and Herald®, 2000), 225.

RANKO STEFANOVIC

Chapter 15

Does God Know the Future?

Wouldn't it be good to know the future? If people had some knowledge of the future, how many decisions would be made differently? How many problems could be avoided? How many disasters could be prevented?

Since earliest times, human beings have been intrigued by the question of what will happen in the future—to them personally, to their kingdoms, or to humanity in general. Many ancient nations developed whole systems of predicting the future. And now, with the new millennium, the fascination with the future captures people's minds more than ever before. As in the past, people today are intrigued by questions about what the future will bring to them.

The end of the world is a common subject these days. Not long ago this was a subject that only religious people talked about, but today "it is the concern of every thinking person."[1] The reason for this is the current situation in the world, characterized by issues such as climate change, world population growth, a failing global financial system, the threat of terrorist attacks, and moral decay.

The current world situation affirms the relevance of the Christian view of the end of the world. Bible prophecies are becoming meaningful and appealing. The biblical portrayal of the time of the end looks "as timely as the morning paper and the hourly newscast."[2]

At this point, a question might puzzle you: Is it truly possible to know where history is leading? Or, what is the future of this world?

Does God know the future?

He does. A principal tenet of the Bible is that God is able to know beforehand what will occur in the future. Here are some of God's claims: "I am God, and there is none like me," Isaiah spoke on behalf of God, "I make known the end from the beginning, from ancient times, what is still to come" (Isaiah 46:9, 10).[3] "I foretold the former things long ago" (Isaiah 48:3; cf. Daniel 2:28). Similarly, Jesus stated, "I am telling you now before it happens, so that when it does happen you will believe that I am who I am" (John 13:19; cf. 14:29). The Bible is replete with similar statements referring to divine foreknowledge.

Someone may ask, How reliable are these biblical claims? In trying to find the answer to this question, it is essential to first understand how God experiences time, since our questions regarding whether or not God knows the future come out of our own human experience of time.

No human analogy can adequately explain the mystery of God. However, some illustrations may be helpful to explain God's relation to time. The biblical concept of time is best explained as a line moving forward from past to future towards its final goal. Human beings find themselves confined to that time line, traveling from one point to the next. All they experience is the present as it happens. They cannot see the future.

This biblical concept stands in contrast to the Greek circular concept of time. Ancient Greeks viewed time as a recurring circle in which history repeats itself. In this concept, history is going nowhere. It is actually the past that defines the future. Thus, the future has no significance because the future is only a recurrence of the past.

So how does God fit into the picture? It has been suggested that if time is a line along which we travel from the present to the future, God may adequately be pictured as the whole page on which the line is drawn. God is outside the time line. He is above time. His realm is eternity, and He is able to see the future as we see the present.

In such a way, God does not foresee or anticipate the things to happen in the future; He simply sees them happening. The future to Him is as real as the present. While we experience only the present on the time line, He experiences the future events as if they are already taking place.[4]

Since God is able to see what will happen in the future, He finds it good to reveal some of it to us. This revelation of future history to human beings in the Bible is referred to as prophecy.

The reliability of biblical prophecy

Prophecy comprises a large part of the Bible. While most of the biblical content consists exclusively of God's messages addressing the present situation of people, the prophetic sections, in most cases, extend beyond that current and local situation. These important parts of God's message provide an insight into the future.

Hundreds of predictive prophecies are evident confirmations of the divine inspiration of the Bible. Biblical prophecy does not belong to the category of other religious books such as the Koran, the Confucian

Analects, the alleged predictions of Nostradamus, and others. Only the Bible manifests evidences of many fulfilled prophecies that affirm its divine origin.

Many biblical prophecies were fulfilled long after the prophetic writer had passed away. For example, the prophet Jeremiah predicted that the Jews would spend seventy years in Babylonian captivity, after which the Persian king would give them authority to rebuild Jerusalem and the temple, which were about to be destroyed (2 Chronicles 36:22, 23; cf. Jeremiah 29:10). Almost a century before he appeared on the scene, Isaiah predicted that the name of that Persian king would be Cyrus (Isaiah 44:28).

In 603 B.C., Daniel predicted that there would be four world empires to appear successively on the world scene: Babylon, Medo-Persia, Greece, and Rome (Daniel 2; 7), embracing a period of more than one thousand years in history. Daniel further prophesied that the Roman Empire would be followed by divided nations (Daniel 2:41–43) dominated by an oppressive religious-political power through the medieval period to the establishment of God's kingdom (Daniel 7:23–25).

These prophecies were literally and ultimately fulfilled centuries later. Despite the consistent efforts by some to undermine the reliability of these prophecies, the overwhelming evidence of their authenticity, along with their precise fulfillment, continues to fill many thinking skeptics with amazement.

In addition, many Messianic prophecies were fulfilled at the first coming of Christ. Centuries before Jesus the Messiah was born, the prophets had predicted, for instance, that He would come out of the tribe of Judah (Genesis 49:10), be born in Bethlehem (Micah 5:2), would bear human sins (Isaiah 53:4, 11, 12), die a substitutionary death (Isaiah 53:5, 12), win ultimate victory over Satan by His death (Genesis 3:15), be resurrected (Psalm 16:10), and be exalted on the heavenly throne (Psalm 110:1). Daniel also prophesied that the Messiah would come 483 years after the Persian king issued an edict allowing the Jews to rebuild Jerusalem (Daniel 9:24–27), which then lay in ruins.

The Bible also contains prophecies still waiting to be fulfilled. The certainty of their fulfillment is guaranteed: (1) by the biblical claim that God knows the future, and (2) by the prophecies already fulfilled in the past. That is why we can say that "we have the prophetic message as something completely reliable" (2 Peter 1:19).

Why we need biblical prophecy

The Bible provides the best answer to the question of why we need biblical prophecy. There we find two analogies of biblical prophecy.

Prophecy is identified as a lamp shining during a dark time until the dawning of the day (2 Peter 1:19). A lamplike prophecy shows us where we are now, as well as where we are going. It also tells us where this world is going and what the conclusion of its history will be. We will need prophetic guidance until the arising of the "Morning Star," Jesus Christ Himself (Revelation 22:16). Then we will have no further need of this lamplike prophetic word (1 Corinthians 13:8–10).

Prophecy is also compared to a mirror by which we can see the future dimly (1 Corinthians 13:12). In Paul's time, mirrors were made of highly polished brass, giving an imperfect reflection of the image. Similarly, biblical prophecy gives a pale presentation of the future, described in an imperfect human language. But when reality comes, "we shall see face to face. Now I know in part; then I shall know fully" (1 Corinthians 13:12).

This dim aspect of biblical prophecy is expressed in peculiar language, not always easy to interpret. The real end-time events in Revelation are not portrayed in straightforward language but in symbols. The understanding of the meaning of these symbols will give us the key for unlocking and decoding their meaning as intended by God.

What prophecy tells us about the end time

End-time prophecies, particularly those recorded in Revelation, inform us about *what* will happen in the world at the time of the end. The Bible states that God "does nothing without revealing his plan to his servants the prophets" (Amos 3:7). Prophecy reveals those things that will happen at the end of time, that are profitable for our salvation and entry into God's kingdom. Its purpose is to tell us, from Heaven's perspective, why and how the events at the time of the end are going to happen. God has revealed in the prophetic word all future events important for us to know. For this reason, two things must be kept in mind.

First of all, predictive prophecies, whether already fulfilled or yet to happen, are not themselves the primary goal. They seem to have a deeper purpose. Their graphic portrayal, as bizarre and frightening as it might look, is not used to intimidate us, but to help us get ready for the end. Prophecies are intended to make us better Christians, to help us take this life seriously, and to inspire us to try to reach people around us with the gospel message for the kingdom.

Second, end-time prophecies are not recorded to make the Bible a kind of a divine horoscope or a fortune-telling book. They are not given to satisfy our obsessive curiosity about the future. Their purpose is rather to assure us that God holds the future. He knows what the future brings and He will be with His faithful people "always, to the very end of the age" (Matthew 28:20). "When these things begin to take place," Jesus said, "lift up your heads, because your redemption is drawing near" (Luke 21:28).

What prophecy does not tell us about the end time

A caution is necessary here. While prophecy tells us what will happen at the time of the end, there are clearly two things that prophecy does not reveal regarding end-time events.

First, it does not tell us exactly *when* end-time events will happen or *when* the end will come. Jesus made it very clear that the exact time of the end is known only to God (Matthew 24:36). He repeatedly stressed that the date of His coming was not revealed to any person on earth.[5] Nobody has been given the ability "to know the times or dates the Father has set by his own authority" (Acts 1:7). The New Testament is replete with affirmations that the exact time of the end is not given to us to know.[6] The exact fulfillment of the end-time events will be the clear indication to us that the end has come and that Christ is "at the door" (Matthew 24:33).

Second, prophecy does not tell us exactly *how* end-time events will take place. The manner of the unfolding of the final events is a secret that God has reserved for Himself. "The secret things belong to the Lord our God, but the things revealed belong to us and to our children forever, that we may follow all the words of this law" (Deuteronomy 29:29).

Books have been written and Web pages created endeavoring to explain how end-time events will take place. However, most of the ideas expressed are misleading, for they are drawn, not from the Bible, but rather from human speculation based on allegorical imagination and newspaper articles.[7]

Exactly *when* and *how* the final events will take place will be ultimately clear at the time of their fulfillment, not before (cf. John 14:29; 16:4).

How to know that the end has come

The ultimate fulfillment of biblical prophecy will be realized with the second coming of Christ. The Second Coming is the event that marks the conclusion of this word's history and, at the same time, the beginning of God's eternal kingdom, free of all evil and injustice that cause pain and death.

While Christ promised to come back, He did not indicate the exact time of His return. We must not, therefore, involve ourselves with speculations either about the date of His coming or the sequential events to precede it.

While prophecy does not reveal the exact time of Christ's coming, Jesus stated that signs will show that is near (cf. Matthew 24:4–14). These signs will be evident in all spheres: natural, political/social, moral, and religious; however, they are not to be understood as indications that the end has arrived.

The intensification of these signs in the natural and the political/social world, together with the deterioration of moral and religious conditions, will eventually reach a point unprecedented in this earth's history. At the same time, there will be specific events, as portrayed in Revelation 13–16. "These events—with decayed world conditions and the worldwide proclamation of the gospel—will be the clear indication of the imminence of Christ's coming."[8]

As we wait for that day, it is important to keep a balance between the future and the present. While prophecy informs us of what the future will bring, it also constantly reminds us of the fact that we are still here, and it urges us to readiness and active waiting.

Until that day, we must pay attention to the most reliable lamplike prophecy shining in this dark time of history, as we wait in confidence for the daybreak, knowing that Jesus Himself has promised to be with us always (Matthew 28:29). When the Morning Star, Jesus Himself, will appear, we will see Him face to face (2 Peter 1:19).

For further reading:

Doukhan, Jacques B. *Secrets of Daniel*. Hagerstown, Md.: Review and Herald®, 2000.

Paulien, Jon. *What the Bibles Says About the End-Time*. Hagerstown, Md.: Review and Herald®, 1994.

Stefanovic, Ranko. *Revelation of Jesus Christ*. 2nd ed. Berrien Springs, Mich.: Andrews University Press, 2009.

Stefanovic, Zdravko. *Daniel: Wisdom to the Wise*. Nampa, Idaho: Pacific Press®, 2007.

Ranko Stefanovic *is a professor of the New Testament in the Adventist Theological Seminary, Andrews University. He earned his PhD in New Testament from Andrews University in 1995, with an emphasis on the book of Revelation. Prior to his graduate studies, he served for eighteen years as an ordained Seventh-day Adventist minister in his home country of what used to be Yugoslavia. After completing doctoral studies, he chaired the Department of Religious Studies at the Canadian University College from 1996 to 1999. From 1999 to 2009, he taught in the undergraduate religion department at Andrews University. He has authored* Revelation of Jesus Christ, *a highly popular commentary on the book of Revelation, which is the standard textbook in many Adventist colleges and universities. He and his wife, Estera, have two grown children.*

References

¹ Richard Rice, *The Reign of God*, 2nd ed. (Berrien Springs, Mich.: Andrews University Press, 2005), 320.

² Ibid., 320, 321.

³ Bible quotations are from Today's New International Version

⁴ C. S. Lewis, *Mere Christianity* (New York: Harper Collins, 1952; reprint 2001), 168–170.

⁵ Matthew 24:36–44, 50; 25:13; Luke 12:40.

⁶ That is, 1 Thessalonians 5:2–4; 2 Peter 3:3–7, 10; Revelation 16:15.

⁷ See Ranko Stefanovic, *Revelation of Jesus Christ*, 2nd ed. (Berrien Springs, Mich.: Andrews University Press, 2009), 1.

⁸ Ranko Stefanovic, "The Second Coming of Christ," *Ministry*, December 2004, 8. This section of the chapter is an abstract from that article.

BRUCE L. BAUER

Chapter 16

Aren't All Religions Basically the Same?

Ours is an age when it is politically correct to live and let live, to not push our points of view on others, and to be tolerant and accepting. These same attitudes have spilled over into the religious areas of life, with many voicing the opinion that all religions are basically the same so it really doesn't matter what you believe. But are all religions really the same? Let's examine the beliefs of the world religions with the largest numbers of followers.

New Age movement

The New Age movement has great diversity, but basic to most followers is the idea that each person is divine. It has two different concepts of God. Many believe in a monistic view of God and see God's essence and the world's essence as one and the same—God is an impersonal oneness. Whereas the second view, pantheism, views God not as a personality, but everything in the universe as part of the Divine. Everything is connected to and emanates from that divine oneness.

New Age followers believe that the problem with humanity is one of perception instead of sin. People have forgotten that they are connected to and emanate from God, which is a universal mind. They believe there is nothing people can do to separate themselves from the divine oneness. The human problem is not rebellion but ignorance of who the true self is, so New Agers promote the concept of self-help and self-achievement through meditation, yoga, and an emphasis on health.

New Age teachings stress that human beings in their true nature are unconditionally connected to the Divine. Ignorance of one's divinity, together with the consequences resulting from this ignorance, cause problems for people. Sin is not the human problem, for everyone is morally innocent, perfect, and divine in their true nature.

New Agers are encouraged to seek out avatars, gurus, enlightened masters, or spirit guides to assist them in their spiritual transformations. Jesus is often seen as just one of many avatars or a manifestation of someone who realized His divine nature, which resulted in His enlightenment.

The ultimate goal for each person is to relinquish all attachments with the personal ego and merge with the ultimate reality or universal oneness.

Hinduism

Hinduism has developed into a rich pluralistic religion with a great variety of worship forms, customs, gods and goddesses, theologies, and philosophies. Hinduism is a religious culture with many ways of expressing the sacred.

Hindus believe in the impersonal essence of God, and whereas they may worship many gods, Hindus believe that all gods are essentially one.

Whereas Judaism, Christianity, and Islam stress the difference between the divine and human nature, Hinduism sees humanity as an integral part of the divine essence—all are part of the one essence, and any perceived difference is a result of ignorance.

Hindus consider the nature of humanity to be divine in its essence. They would suggest that human beings face numerous reincarnations in an illusionary world due to their bad *karma* and ignorance, for people have forgotten that they are an extension of Brahman and have attached themselves to the desires of their egos. If people suffer because of sickness, hunger, or disaster, it is because of their own evil actions and bad karma in a previous life.

Salvation is described as deliverance from the almost endless cycles of reincarnation, and this can be attained through *jnana* (knowledge, insight, and wisdom), *karma* (action or works), or *bhakti* (ecstatic devotion). A person's final state or goal is the liberation from these cycles of births and rebirths and the merging with ultimate reality or heavenly bliss in the presence of the gods.

Hinduism is very different from other world religions because there is no unified system of beliefs, no doctrine of salvation, and no centralized authority.

Buddhism

The original Buddhist doctrine did not entail any concept of God; however, later sects introduced some godly figures. Neither do Buddhists worship the Buddha (Siddhartha Gautama). It is believed that Buddha discovered the way while meditating to attain spiritual enlightenment and escape from the endless cycles of births and rebirths. Thus, he is called the enlightened one.

Always Prepared

Buddhism attributes suffering to ignorance of the four noble truths, which state that (1) life consists of suffering, (2) everything is impermanent, (3) the way to escape suffering is to eliminate all desire, and (4) desire can be eliminated by following the eightfold path. Buddhists do not believe that people are sinful, nor have they offended a holy, perfect God, nor are they seen as in rebellion against God.

I was teaching a Bible class to a group of Japanese college students. We had been studying for several weeks, and, on that particular night, I was teaching about sin. Towards the end of the presentation, I made the statement, "We are all sinners, right?" and received a lot of blank looks. Feeling that perhaps they had not understood my question I asked it in Japanese. *"Watakushi takushi wa minna sumibito desu, ne?"* But instead of getting the agreement that I expected, they all shook their heads, "no." We sang a song and had a quick closing prayer. Then I started to explore what the Japanese Buddhist understanding of the word *sumi* or "sin" means in their language. What I found was fascinating.

The typical Buddhist Japanese thinks of a sinner as someone who has committed some terrible offense such as murder, and who has been caught and is now being led off in handcuffs to prison. That was their view of sin, so when I said, "We are all sinners, right?" they were totally confused. As soon as I understood the Buddhist definition of sin, I then went on to pour the Christian and biblical meaning of sin into their Japanese word. I taught that the biblical concept included all that the Japanese concept of *sumi* entailed, plus selfishness, plus the idea of not being absolutely perfect, plus offense against the Creator God. What we ended up with was a subgroup of people who understood *sumi*, but not in the traditional Japanese sense. They had added biblical content to the word and now viewed the word in a broader sense with Christian meanings attached.

In Buddhism, human beings are viewed as an impermanent collection of aggregates that are ruled by the iron law of *karma,* which states that you reap what you sow. If you do good, you get good; if you do evil, you get evil. It is also believed that *karma* determines a person's destiny in the next reincarnated life.

The ultimate goal in Buddhism is to enter the state of *nirvana* where the ego is extinguished and the self overcomes the yearnings for sensual desires.

Islam

Muslims believe in one singular God, Allah. They hold a strongly monotheistic view that allows for God to have no partner or for any duality to be associated with Him. They are very critical of the Christian view of the Trinity and some believe that Christians worship God the Father, who had sexual relations with Mary, resulting in a son, Jesus Christ.

Muslims believe that everything that happens is because Allah wills it—nothing happens outside of Allah's will and purpose. This view is grounded in a high view of Allah's sovereignty, with total control over everything that occurs.

Muslims believe that the problem with humanity is that they have rejected right guidance. Sin can be forgiven through repentance, but no atonement is necessary. To be a good Muslim, one must (1) repeat the creed that states that there is one God and Muhammad is His prophet, (2) recite prayers in Arabic five times a day, (3) give alms to the poor, (4) fast from food, drink, sex, and smoking during the month of Ramadan, and (5) make a pilgrimage to Mecca at least once during one's lifetime.

Muslims honor Jesus as one of the greatest prophets, but they do not believe He is God. They also do not believe that He died on the cross, but rather that Judas took His place while Jesus was taken to heaven without dying. Muslims feel strongly that Allah would never allow an honored prophet to suffer such a horrible death. Muslims also believe that Jesus will come to this earth a second time to judge the world.

The basis of that final judgment largely depends on a person's good deeds and religious faithfulness to the duties required of a follower of Allah. However, Allah, in His mercy, can forgive whomever He chooses. The Koran begins many *surahs* (chapters) by stressing that Allah is most merciful. Muslims strive to have their good deeds outweigh their evil deeds, but ultimately salvation is a gift from Allah that is obtained through righteous living and Allah's mercy on Judgment Day. Salvation means to enter Paradise, whereas those who do not measure up will face eternity in hell.

Christianity

Christians believe in a personal God who wants to be known. From the very beginning of God's relationship with human beings, words such as family, community, adoption, sons and daughters, and friends have been used in the Bible to describe God's desire for fellowship and relationship with people. The focus in Christianity is not on performing good works or following religious rituals in order to achieve salvation, but on living in a loving relationship with Jesus Christ and trusting (having faith) in His death as an atoning sacrifice for each person's sins.

Christianity takes sin much more seriously than any other religion. Sin, as defined in the Bible, is much more than human ignorance, wrong desires, or the rejections of right guidance. Sin, even one little sin, is much more deadly in that it eternally separates people from God with no possibility for a human solution. Christians believe that sin results in death, both the death we see all around us, but also what the Bible calls the second death that occurs at the end of the world's history when all people will face God's judgment. Those who have rejected the death of Jesus Christ as a substitute for their second death will be eternally destroyed.

This is where the significance of Jesus Christ comes into the picture. The focus is on Jesus Christ Himself, not just His teachings. No other religious leader ever claimed to be sinless—the Buddha said the problem was bad *karma* that would require endless cycles of reincarnation to overcome and Muhammad admitted his own failures. In contrast, Jesus said that He was the way, the only way to return to God. Some have seen this statement (John 14:6) as arrogant and much too narrow for modern attitudes of inclusiveness. But if sin is as deadly as the Bible says it is, and is more than ignorance or wrong desires, then, a much more radical solution is needed than just better understanding, right desires, or careful obedience. The way Jesus provided to overcome the sin problem is wide enough for the whole world. His death paid the penalty for sin, not His own sin, for He lived a sinless life, but for anyone who believes and trusts in His sacrificial death. Instead of struggling to perform good works or striving for good *karma* Christians live in a faith relationship with God, trusting in what Christ did on the cross to provide forgiveness and the possibility of living for eternity with a loving, caring God.

Great diversity in the world's religions

Let's go back to the question we asked at the beginning of the chapter—aren't all religions basically the same? As we have seen, the various religions have very different views of the human problem and how to solve it. New Agers see the problem as ignorance, Islam considers it as a failure to obediently follow God's guidance, Buddhism says the problem is wrong desires, Hinduism blames bad *karma* in previous lives, and Christianity sees it as sin that eternally separates us from God.

The various religions also have great differences when it comes to belief about God. "It is really ludicrous to suppose that all religions lead to God, when Buddhism does not believe that there is any God at all, when Islam makes him so far removed, when Hinduism offers extinction after many incarnations and in the meantime sanctions idolatry on a massive scale. How can all religions lead to God when they have such different beliefs about God, the afterlife and how one can attain it?"[1]

The solutions offered by the various religions also differ. New Agers suggest that right thinking that allows people to understand that they are already divine is all that is needed. Hinduism allows at least three ways for people to achieve enlightenment—through the way of action and ritual, through the way of knowledge and meditation, and through the way of devotion. Buddhists believe that the way to overcome all desire is to follow the middle path between extreme affluence and extreme asceticism and to accrue *karmic* merit. Muslims believe that faithfulness in religious duty and obedience coupled with Allah's forgiveness and mercy is the solution to the sin problem, whereas Christians believe that sin can only be forgiven by the shed blood of Jesus Christ.

Though it is possible to find many similarities among the world's religions, a closer look will reveal irreconcilable differences among their most basic teachings. Many people believe that the religions differ on the surface, but, on a deeper level, they are the same. In fact, the opposite is true: the religions are similar on the surface level, but on the deeper level—the level of their fundamental beliefs and teachings—they are very different.[2]

All religions meet some of the basic yearnings of the human heart. All religions answer many of the questions asked by people. But all religions are not the same; they do not even have similar views of God, sin, the ultimate destiny, or the way to achieve that destiny. When people suggest that all religions are basically the same, it may be that they have never seriously considered the above differences and are only trying to be politically correct, both of which are very inadequate criteria to which one might entrust one's ultimate destiny.

The basic element lacking in all other religions is the clear and correct understanding of the Person of Jesus. Only through Him are human beings able to order their lives so that they may walk with Him in eternal glory.

For further reading:

Adamson, Marilyn. "Connecting With the Divine: Descriptions of the World's Major Religions: Hinduism, Buddhism, Islam, Christianity, and New Age." Accessed February 1, 2010. http://www.everystudent.com/features/connecting.html.

Green, Michael. *"But Don't All Religions Lead to God?": Navigating the Multi-faith Maze.* Grand Rapids, Mich.: Baker Books, 2002.

Halverson, Dean C., ed. *The Compact Guide to World Religions.* Minneapolis, Minn.: Bethany House, 1996.

Witmer, Daryl E. "Aren't All Religions Basically the Same?" Accessed February 1, 2010. http://christiananswers.net/q-aiia/religionssame.html.

Bruce L. Bauer. *After graduating with a BA in theology in 1969, Bruce and his wife, Linda, traveled to Osaka, Japan, where they worked with the Seventh-day Adventist English Language Schools coordinating the service of hundreds of student missionaries. After fifteen years, the Bauers moved to Guam, where Bruce was president of the Guam-Micronesia Mission for five years. During furloughs, Bruce earned an MA in religion from Andrews University in 1975, an MA in missiology from Fuller Theological Seminary in 1981, and a DMiss from Fuller in 1983. From 1989 until 1997, Bauer taught at the Seventh-day Adventist Theological Seminary, then spent three and a half years as president of the Cambodia Adventist Mission. He returned to Andrews University in January of 2001, where he chairs the Department of World Mission and edits the* Journal of Adventist Mission Studies.

References

[1] Michael Green, *"But Don't All Religions Lead to God?": Navigating the Multi-faith Maze* (Grand Rapids, Mich.: Baker Books, 2002), 22.

[2] Dean C. Halverson, ed., *The Compact Guide to World Religions* (Minneapolis, Minn.: Bethany House, 1996), 241, 242.

PAUL DYBDAHL

Chapter 17

Does It Really Matter What I Believe as Long as I Am Sincere?

In today's world, there is doubt about the importance of believing specific doctrines. People look for what is right for them, for what "feels good." Thus, values differ.

The times and places of our births have profound effects on the values that we will adopt and hold dear. In some cultures, hospitality and loyalty are key values. In other places, courage and purity might be viewed with greater admiration. In yet a different setting, the qualities of duty or perseverance or patriotism might be more highly esteemed.

The value of sincerity

From my vantage point as a professor in a Christian university, it seems that one of the values gaining popularity both locally and globally is the value of sincerity. According to the dictionary, one who is sincere is "marked by genuineness" and an "absence of hypocrisy."[1] Among the young people with whom I work, there is a growing consensus that thoughtful, loving people should not get caught up in needless debates over differing beliefs and views of truth. "After all, since we will never agree, why bother?" many would say. "What really counts is that we are sincere and honest about what we believe."

Just recently, this perspective was reinforced by students in two of my religion classes. When asked to rank the qualities that God would most want to see in us, university students overwhelmingly said that God valued our sincerity more than He desired purity or orthodoxy. But is this really the case?

I would agree that there is something comforting about the notion that what someone believes or the purity of his or her life doesn't matter as long as the person is sincere. Such a view sounds open-minded, inclusive, and sensitive (which are also values that are currently surging in popularity). It is also true that one could even turn to the Bible to show the value of sincerity.

In 1 Chronicles, David urged his son Solomon to "acknowledge the God of your father, and serve him with wholehearted devotion" (28:9).[2] The earliest believers in Jesus are described as meeting and eating together "with glad and sincere hearts" (Acts 2:46). In 1 Timothy, sincerity is one of the necessary requirements for church leaders (3:8). Finally, in James, wisdom from heaven is described as "impartial and sincere" (3:17). Beyond these explicit references, the Bible is filled with stories that demonstrate the value of sincerity and wholeheartedness before God. One of Jesus' greatest criticisms of the religious leaders of His day was that they were hypocrites and lacked sincerity (see, e.g., Matthew 23:13, 15, 23, 25, 27, 28).

It is clear, then, that sincerity is indeed an admirable quality that God would desire for all of us. It is also true that our salvation doesn't depend on our mental assent to all the correct beliefs. God can save sincere people who may be ignorant or confused about what is right and true. But does that mean that what a person believes doesn't matter as long as they are sincere? Is it reasonable to elevate sincerity to the point that we could conclude that what we believe *does not matter as long as we are sincere*?

Some limitations of sincerity

From my perspective, this elevation of the quality of sincerity often overlooks two features of sincerity. First of all, being truly sincere is much more difficult than we may at first suppose. The appeal to sincerity rather than correct belief is *not* a movement away from ambiguity to peaceful confidence. Instead of making things simpler or easier, the call to sincerity is an incredibly high standard that poses a problem for us.

Our deceitful hearts

According to Jeremiah 17:9, "The heart is deceitful above all things and beyond cure. Who can understand it?" If the sinful human heart is so deceitful, perhaps our retreat from debates over "beliefs" and "truth" to the safety of sincerity may not be safe. Even if sincerity was all that mattered, how could we know whether or not we were fully sincere? It is a sort of slippery virtue, one that is difficult to fully and consistently possess or even define.

How many times have we thought we were sincere about something, only to realize later that we had deceived ourselves and that our motives were not as pure as we had first believed? For example, marriages typically begin with two people who honestly feel that they have found their soul mate. They willingly take vows of fidelity and love and pledge faithfulness to each other for the rest of their lives. They are sincere. However, if we were to visit those couples a few years later, we would find that some of the marriages had already ended. Further conversation would bring about a confession from many that, in hindsight, they now recognize that they got married at least partly to please parents, ease loneliness, satisfy their desire for physical intimacy, avoid problems at home, or perhaps even to enjoy increased financial security. If someone had suggested this to them at the wedding, they would have vehemently—and sincerely—denied that this was the case. Their motivations were present yet subconscious, so, at the time, they could not even see that their decision and their vows were less than totally sincere. Clearly, our human judgments about sincerity are not very trustworthy.

Can sincerity stand alone?

The question, Does it really matter what I believe as long as I am sincere? may also arise from the assumption that sincerity is a stand-alone quality that can exist apart from belief. Actually, this is not the case at all.

Sincerity presupposes a belief in or about something. This reality is demonstrated in a number of biblical passages that use the word *sincere*. The apostle Paul, writing to believers in Corinth, confesses that he is afraid their "minds may somehow be led astray from your sincere and pure devotion *to Christ*" (2 Corinthians. 11:3).[3] Notice that sincerity has an object—Christ. In 2 Timothy 1:5, it is "sincere *faith*"; in 1 Peter 1:22, it is "sincere *love for your brothers.*"

So, to the person who says, "I am sincere," we should rightly ask, "Sincere about what?" He or she could be sincere in the belief that sincerity does not matter. Someone might even be sincere in their belief that they are not sincere! If it sounds confusing, that is the point. Sincerity must be attached to something in order for it to mean something. It is impossible to be sincere without being sincere about something, and that means sincerity and belief cannot be separated.

The importance of belief

This leads to what I think is the most glaring problem with the statement that what one believes doesn't matter as long as he or she is sincere. The problem is simply this: *beliefs do matter because what we believe guides our behavior.* The connection between belief and behavior—and the importance of that connection—can be illustrated by an almost unlimited number of examples.

On April 26, 1986, the Chernobyl nuclear reactor in the Soviet Union released radiation that killed more than four thousand people and ultimately disabled more than seventy thousand others. The cause of the disaster was not a lack of sincerity on the part of the Soviet nuclear experts. Instead, they were testing one of Chernobyl's four reactors and honestly, wholeheartedly believed they would be able to control the rate of fission. They were wrong. An uncontrolled chain reaction took place and the reactor exploded. The experts were not evil people. They were not trying to poison the environment and kill their families and the townspeople living nearby. They were sincere. But their sincerity did not protect them from the drastic consequences of their misguided belief that eight boron-carbide rods would be enough to control the nuclear chain reaction.[4]

Those acquainted with medical history are aware that even into the first half of the 1800s, well-meaning doctors regularly examined and treated patient after patient without washing their hands. They used instruments that had not been sterilized and wore the same surgical gown throughout the day, despite the buildup of blood and pus from prior procedures. These doctors were sincere in their desires to help patients, but they did not understand how infections were transmitted. It was not surprising, then, that deadly infections spread wildly among those who had undergone surgery. Amputations had a mortality rate of between 40 to 45 percent. Puerperal fever (an infection of the uterus at the time of childbirth) killed nearly one in five new mothers in some hospitals.[5]

How many of us today would want one of those surgeons operating on us? How many of us would say, "Well, as long as the doctor is sincere, I don't care what they believe about the transmission of infection—or about human anatomy, even. What they believe doesn't matter!" Would we say the same thing about a pilot ("It doesn't matter if they believe the air traffic controller, as long as they sincerely want to fly me back home")? How about a teacher or a preacher? We certainly want them to be sincere, but we also want something more.

In every area of our daily lives, we expect people to be aware of the knowledge that is available to them. We want them to be informed so that they will then be able to behave accordingly. In short, we expect them to know and believe that which is reasonable and then sincerely live in harmony with those beliefs. To do otherwise is irresponsible—even foolish.

The same thing is true in the realm of religion and faith. Missiologist K. P. Yohannon tells the story of a trader who landed on one of the islands of the South Pacific for the first time. As this merchant began to talk with the chief of the island, he noticed a Bible in the chief's home and realized that missionaries had already visited the island. In disgust, the merchant mocked the chief, saying, " 'What a shame . . . that you have listened to this foolish nonsense of the missionaries.' " The chief faced the trader and said, " 'Do you see the large white stone over there? That is a stone where just a few years ago we used to smash the heads of our victims to get at their brains. Do you see that large oven over there? That is the oven where just a few years ago we used to bake the bodies of our victims before we feasted upon them. Had we not listened to what you call the nonsense of those missionaries, I assure you that your head would already be smashed on that rock and your body would be baking in that oven.' "[6]

What made the difference for the chief? I suspect that we would agree that there was a positive change in the chief's life, but that change didn't involve a movement from hypocrisy to sincerity. He may have smashed skulls and cooked brains with great sincerity! Instead, the difference came when his beliefs changed, and those new beliefs led to a profound and positive change in behavior.

One need not look far to find people today who are fervently, sincerely devoted to a religious ideology. Their sincerity is admirable, but their beliefs may lead them to actions such as strapping explosives onto their bodies and then detonating those explosives in the middle of unsuspecting crowds. Jesus Himself warned against blind religious passion when He told His disciples that the day would come "when anyone who kills you will think he is offering a service to God" (John 16:2). Sincerity certainly is not enough. What we believe matters. It matters to us, it matters to others, and it matters to God.

Throughout the Bible, we see God's efforts to carefully instruct His followers on the best way to live. As the psalmist said, "I will never forget your precepts, for by them you have preserved my life," and "Your word is a lamp to my feet and a light for my path" (Psalm 119:93, 105). It may not always be easy to understand God's guidance. Believers will not always agree on every point of doctrine, but we are expected to prayerfully and humbly search the Scriptures so that we can stand as one who "does not need to be ashamed and who correctly handles the word of truth" (2 Timothy 2:15). The struggle to rightfully understand God's guidance is worth it. The more we understand God's will for us, the better we will be able to live.

The life of belief and sincerity

In 1 Peter 1:21, 22, the importance of belief, obedience, and sincerity are drawn together in a beautiful unity. There, the apostle Peter writes to the church, reminding them that through Christ, "you believe in God." Peter then continues, "Now that you have purified yourselves by obeying the truth so that you have sincere love for your brothers, love one another deeply, from the heart."

I believe Peter would make the same appeal to us. May our belief in God lead to obedience, which will then be expressed in sincere, heartfelt love for others. If we lived like this, we would be happier, better people. The world would be a happier, better place too.

For further reading:

Briscoe, Pete. *Belief Matters*. Eugene, Ore.: Harvest House, 2009.

Keller, Timothy. "There Can't Be Just One True Religion." In *The Reason for God*, 3–21. New York: Dutton, 2008.

Sire, James W. *Why Should Anyone Believe Anything at All?* Downers Grove, Ill.: InterVarsity, 1994.

Stott, John R. W. *Your Mind Matters.* Downers Grove, Ill.: InterVarsity, 1972.

White, Ellen G. "A Knowledge of God." In *Steps to Christ*, 89–96. Mountain View, Calif.: Pacific Press®, 1948.

Paul Dybdahl *moved to the Pacific Northwest in 1976, after spending the early years of his life in Asia (Thailand and Singapore). He graduated from Walla Walla College in 1992 and accepted a call as a pastor in the Oregon Conference, where he served for nearly five years. During that time, he earned his MDiv from Andrews University in 1995. Dybdahl returned to Andrews for doctoral studies and earned a PhD in missiology in 2004. Currently, he serves as a professor in the School of Theology at Walla Walla University, where he has been teaching since 2001. Most of his research, presentations, and publications focus on how Christians can effectively communicate the gospel across cultural barriers. He and his wife, Kristyn, have three children: Noah, Alyssa, and Sarah.*

References

[1] *Merriam-Webster Online*, s.v. "Sincere," accessed March 25, 2010, http://www.merriam-webster.com/dictionary/sincere.

[2] All Scripture citations are taken from the New International Version.

[3] In all cases, italics are added for emphasis.

[4] Judith Newman, "20 of the Greatest Blunders in Science in the Last 20 Years," *Discover*, October 1, 2000, accessed April 9, 2010, http://discovermagazine.com/2000/oct/featblunders.

[5] "Antisepsis," Discoveries in Medicine, accessed March 23, 2010, http://www.discoveriesinmedicine.com/A-AN/Antisepsis.html.

[6] K. P. Yohannan, *Revolution in World Missions* (Carrollton, Tex.: GFA Books, 2003), 111, 112.

WOODROW W. WHIDDEN

Chapter 18

How Can I Find Salvation and Eternal Life?

Although this question is often asked by those who have become sensitive to the felt need for God in their lives and hunger for some sort of hope of eternal life in a world threatened by the imminent reality of death, it may be the wrong question. The question that seems to be more reflective of the overall biblical narrative deals not so much with how humans find salvation, but how God's saving grace *finds* us—lost, alienated, sinners.

Traditionally, in the Western world, questions raised about salvation have been posed in terms of freedom from the guilt and power of sin. While young adults in the twenty-first century may not be asking questions about guilt caused by sin, the question of guilt remains a serious fact of human existence. This happens because the Spirit is always reaching out to bring about the conviction of sin.

For me, the key to meaningful human existence revolves around the definitions of the biblical words *sin* and *love*. And it is in the meaning of these words that Christians claim to have discovered the very heart of what salvation means. We shall begin with the positive: love.

Divine love versus sin

The central theme of Scripture reveals that not only is God a being of love at the core of His very nature (1 John 4:8), but that His love is creative and outwardly flowing in setting up worlds where free, intelligent, relational beings (made in God's image) can share His loving relationships. But the tragic subplot of the narrative is that God's love has been severely tested by the open rebellion of both angelic and human beings who have fallen into sin. The good news, however, is that the love that inspired the filling of the universe with loving beings, is up to the task of freely and self-sacrificially restoring these fallen creatures to their original destinies. Moreover, the heart of this entire metanarrative is that God the Father gave His beloved Son to make amazing provisions for the full restoration and healing of the lost human race. This is shown in the beloved text of John 3:16: "For God so loved the world that He gave His only begotten Son, that whoever believes in Him should not perish but have everlasting life."[1]

The really great truth in all of this is that God's love has not only led Him to make provision for human salvation, but it has also led the Triune God to actually take the merciful initiative to communicate these great provisions of Christ to lost, sinful humans—and all of this has been steadily carried out despite persistent human and angelic resistance to the overtures of His love. Thus, with these merciful thoughts of God's loving initiatives in hand, we are now prepared to turn our attention to the problematic word, *sin*.

Normally, this word is closely associated with its two notably horrid offspring—guilt and the prospect of eternal death, allegedly caused by bad actions! Yet the more foundational question that the biblical teaching on sin and salvation seeks to confront has to do with sin's more subtle, even radical ramifications.

Sin has traditionally been defined following a certain interpretation of 1 John 3:4. This interpretation claims that sin is mainly to be defined as an act of transgression that is clearly contrary to the demands of the holy law of God—the Ten Commandments. While this line of interpretation does pinpoint an important facet of sin (bad acts), the Bible strongly suggests that a more visceral definition of sin has to do with the essential badness of human nature itself, not just its bad acts. Christian tradition has referred to this as "total depravity." Ellen White refers to the effects of sin as a defacement and near obliteration of the "image of God" in human beings.[2]

In essence, this more pervasive definition of sin is concerned with a view of human nature that highlights humanity's persistent and infectious selfishness. This insane human preoccupation with self has created a seething caldron from which has bellowed forth the stifling, sulfurous fumes that have generated a profound inner and outer darkness. Moreover, it is from this bellowing blackness of selfishness that all other facets of sin have emerged.

Such a relentlessly enveloping mist has left humanity ensnared in the withering clutches of a power that is inexorably death dealing and distorting. In fact, every definitive aspect of what it means to be human has been perverted—especially our spiritual, moral, and social instincts and aspirations. And when this miasma has reached its nadir, it degenerates into a hell of eternal and final nonexistence.

The apostle Paul has spoken in a most graphic manner regarding the pre-Christian life of the Ephesians: "And you He made alive, who were dead in trespasses and sins, in which you once walked according to the course of this world, according to the prince of the power of the air, the spirit who now works in the sons of disobedience, among whom also we all once conducted ourselves in the lusts of our flesh, fulfilling the desires of the flesh and of the mind, and were by nature children of wrath, just as the others" (Ephesians 2:1–3). This is a most unflattering, sobering description. Its brutal witness, however, evokes a much needed, yet honest analysis of the human condition as it roils in sin.

Please note that the striking impression of this passage features "deadness" in all sorts of bad behavior, driven by the "prince of the power of the air" who is constantly inflaming "the desires of the flesh and of the mind." Is it any wonder that all of humanity is described as being "by nature children of wrath"? And about the only appropriate response is to croak out a groaning, "O wretched man that I am! Who will deliver me from this body of death?" (Romans 7:24; cf. Isaiah 6:5)! So what does it mean practically to be saved from all of this corruption of nature, evil attitudes, and depraved actions?

Freedom from self(ishness): The key to newness of life!

The irreducible core meaning of all of this bad news about human nature speaks to a profound tie-in between inborn sinful nature (especially its inherent selfishness) and the widespread miasma of meaninglessness. Simply put, sin primarily has to do with selfishness and there is no true joy or deep satisfaction in making self-gratification (especially the desires of the carnal lusts) the major business of life! In a wonderfully contrasting manner, there is profound practical truth to be discovered about the salvation that God is offering to sinful humanity: He promises to free us from the hollow promises of selfishness and offers to every responsive human person the wonderfully liberating discovery that life's greatest satisfactions and deepest joys emerge from serving and blessing others, not in the deadening service of self!

So when we say that God saves us from sin by His grace, we mean that He has mounted an all-fronts effort to pull us out of the clutches of selfishness, and to place us on the path to joyous fulfillment as we learn to live lives of other-oriented service. And this comprehensive effort includes deliverance from the entirety of sin's delusive deceptions, guilt, power, and, ultimately, even its very presence in the core of our very natures. Thus, what follows will briefly describe the way that God's grace awakens, forgives, transforms character, and ultimately destroys even the most intractable propensities and inclinations of our depraved natures.

God's way of deliverance from self and sin

The very first phase of God's attempts to draw us away from the deceptions of sin and selfishness is described as calling or awakening grace. The imagery of deadness in Ephesians 2:1 strongly suggests that God's grace is being offered to sinners, whether they want to receive it or not. This is the very first manifestation of God's regenerating or renewing grace. The vivid picture suggested by our deadness in sin is that God is gladly running about in a morgue, banging on coffin lids seeking to awaken the dead! What God graciously does is to arouse minds to the awfulness of sin and the depths of His merciful love for sinners. On our part we simply do not realize how terrible sin is, but when we do begin to get some glimmers of its terribly deranging effects on us, it is only natural to think that God could not love such degraded sinners. So God's awakening grace arouses us to a sense of His undeserved, yet persisting love. At this juncture, the very borders of the new kingdom of love come into view, especially as the gift of repentance comes into play.

This gift of God's "goodness" (Romans 2:4) enables sinners like me to not just despise sin, but also to feel genuinely sorry for sin itself. Moreover, one of the key evidences that any believer's exercise of repentance is genuine is that the excusing of sin ceases, and it is acknowledged and renounced. Furthermore, a hearty confession of both sins and sinfulness will take place!

When we repent, we may know that for Christ's sake we are accepted by God through His forgiving grace. This whole process of regeneration then leads to the new birth, or what is commonly referred to as conversion. Peter said it so succinctly, "Repent therefore and be converted, that your sins may be blotted out" (Acts 3:19). Paul, in one of his more comprehensive comments on this whole process of regeneration and conversion, said, "But God, who is rich in mercy, because of His great love with which He loved us, even when we were dead in trespasses, made us alive together, . . . and made us sit together in heavenly places in Christ Jesus" (Ephesians 2:4–6).

As a believer in Christ I become the beneficiary of the entirety of Christ's redemptive blessings. Therefore, not only does the regenerating work of the Holy Spirit lead to a deeper realization of sinfulness and God's great love (in spite of our sins), but it also alerts responsive believers to the fact that in Christ all subsequent gifts come in Him as one fully wrapped package of salvation. The reference, however, to God being "rich in mercy," points to the forgiveness of sins, or justification by faith alone.

What is God's grace seeking to accomplish in the life of each newly repentant believer? First of all, He saves me from the deceptiveness of sin and the lie that God does not love sinners. This is done in the early stages of regeneration through His awakening grace that draws me into an intimate union with Christ by faith. And one of the immediate fruits of conversion is the gift of forgiveness. Thus, forgiveness frees me from sin's guilt and condemning power. Justification and forgiveness free any sinner who has been united to Christ by faith from the guilt of sin. And when I am freed from sin's guilt, this is the very first and foundational moment when, as a believer, I begin to truly sense my new status of being freed from the power of sin in my life.

The free forgiveness of sins, or justification by faith *alone*, frees us from the burden of trying to win reconciliation with God through good works, often called legalism. In other words, the sincere, but misguided believer can be under the delusion that acts of obedience to any of the requirements of God's will generate merit in his or her behalf. This is simply a delusion of which Paul spoke in the clearest of terms: "For by grace you have been saved through faith, and that not of yourselves, it is the gift of God, not of works, lest anyone should boast. For we are His workmanship, created in Christ Jesus for good works, which God prepared beforehand, that we should walk in them" (Ephesians 2:8–10).

In this passage, Paul easily transitions from converting and justifying faith to transforming or sanctifying faith. Converting and justifying grace free us from the condemnation of sin and the selfishness that thinks it can work its way to heaven. But while Paul taught salvation from the guilt of sin by faith alone, he also made it clear that such a faith will never be alone! Being united to Christ will lead me to change.

Transforming grace or sanctification

This mighty aspect of saving grace is the inward working of God's power that effects a changed character and a nature more and more attuned to the character of Christ. This wonderful grace gradually frees us from sin's dominating power; it is a constant work of Christ that gradually leads to new life. But this is not all! Grace also liberates the mind from improper ideas of sin and righteousness. It thus brings greater clarity regarding the awfulness of sin and the preciousness of God's grace received through faith in Christ. With these changes, my life becomes totally different!

Glorifying grace

The grand finale of transforming grace is the experience of glorification, which happens at the second coming of Jesus, when every true believer will be transformed in both body and mind, freed from any sinful tendencies that may still harass the believer. This will be the finishing touch of deliverance from sin. At this point, my salvation will be complete!

Conclusion

So, how can anyone find salvation? The answer is very simple: by being alert to the gracious workings of the Spirit of God that are constantly communicated to every sinner. This whole attitude can be characterized as a sense of responsiveness to the calling, awakening, and converting grace that arrives as the Spirit seeks to lead from one wonderful stage of regeneration to another. And when I am responsive to the constant outpourings of God's loving grace, having been found by God, I will find salvation in all of its complete and blessed facets. My dear reader, rest assured that God is looking for you. All you need to do is say, "Here I am! Take me and work Your grace in me."

For further reading:

Knight, George. *Sin and Salvation: God's Work for and in Us.* Hagerstown, Md.: Review and Herald®, 2008.

Whidden, Woodrow W. *The Judgment and Assurance: The Dynamics of Personal Salvation.* Hagerstown, Md.: Review and Herald®, 2011.

White, Ellen G. *Steps to Christ.* Any edition.

Woodrow W. Whidden *obtained his PhD at Drew University in 1989, and has served as a pastor and college religion teacher. He recently retired after serving as a seminary professor at the Adventist International Institute of Advanced Studies (AIIAS) in the Philippines. His publications include the books* Salvation *(Review and Herald®, 1995),* The Trinity: Its Implications for Life and Thought *(Review and Herald®, 2002) and* E. J. Waggoner: From the Physician of Good News to Agent of Division *(Review and Herald®, 2008). He is also the coeditor of the book series titled the Library of Adventist Theology, published by the Review and Herald®. He is married to Peggy Gibbs Whidden and they have three children and four grandchildren.*

References

[1] All Bible quotations are from the the New King James Version

[2] Among several references on the topic, see Ellen G. White, *The Great Controversy* (Mountain View, Calif.: Pacific Press®, 1911), 645.

NANCY J. VYHMEISTER

Chapter 19

Why Am I a Seventh-day Adventist?

I am a Seventh-day Adventist because of Jesus Christ. I accept Adventism because it fits into the biblical understanding of who Jesus is, what He did for me, what He asks me to do, and what He will do for me in the future. Having accepted the biblical message about Jesus, I have no choice but to be an Adventist. Let me explain, beginning with those beliefs related to the name of my church. I will then continue with different ways in which membership in the Seventh-day Adventist Church fits in with my belief in Christ.

"Seventh-day Adventist"

Jesus affirmed that He was Lord of the Sabbath (Mark 2:28). Throughout the Bible, Sabbath observance points to Jesus. In the fourth commandment of Exodus 20, the reason given for keeping the day is to remember Creation; according to Colossians 1:16, "By him all things were created."[1] In the Deuteronomy 5 version of the command to keep the Sabbath, the Sabbath is a reminder of liberation from slavery (verse 15);

John 8:32 tells me that Christ makes me free. The Sabbath is the symbol of rest, from its first mention in Genesis 2, where God rests or ceases from His creation work, on to Hebrews 4:9, 10, where the Sabbath is a foretaste of the eternal rest of the saved. And, of course, Jesus is the great Giver of rest: "Come to me, all who labor and are heavy laden, and I will give you rest" (Matthew 11:28).

An Adventist is one who believes in and awaits the second coming of Jesus. Even before His death and resurrection, Jesus promised His disciples: "I go and prepare a place for you, I will come again" (John 14:3). As the disciples, dumbfounded, watched their Lord ascend to heaven, two heavenly messengers gave them the renewed promise: "This Jesus, who was taken up from you into heaven, will come in the same way as you saw him go into heaven" (Acts 1:11).

The person and work of Jesus

Adventist Fundamental Beliefs,[2] in agreement with John 1:1, point to Christ as God, not only the Word "with God." He is a Member of the "heavenly trio," as Ellen White calls the Trinity.[3] As God in human flesh, Jesus could say to Philip: "Whoever has seen me has seen the Father" (John 14:9).

The four Gospels narrate the birth, life, ministry, and death of Jesus. Their story is vital to my belief because it culminates in the crucifixion and resurrection of Jesus. The tomb could not retain Him. On the third day, Jesus arose from the grave, glorious and victorious (Matthew 28:2, 3).

Jesus is my Savior. The apostles preached, "And there is salvation in no one else, for there is no other name under heaven given among men by which we must be saved" (Acts 4:12). Paul wrote to the Ephesians:

"In him we have redemption through his blood, the forgiveness of our trespasses, according to the riches of his grace" (Ephesians 1:7). Furthermore, because of the transaction at the cross, "There is therefore now no condemnation for those who are in Christ Jesus" (Romans 8:1). These biblical teachings about Jesus, and basic to Adventism, lead me to be an Adventist.

According to the book of Hebrews (see especially Hebrews 4:14–16; 8:1–5; 9:11–27; 10:19–22), while Jesus is waiting to return to gather His people, He is the High Priest in the heavenly sanctuary. There He is my Mediator, my Advocate. While some may construe the heavenly judgment as a threat to their happiness, I have nothing to fear from the judgment because Jesus is on my side. I rejoice that Jesus is my High Priest, Advocate, and Judge (2 Timothy 4:1).

A life of obedience

Jesus clearly commissioned His followers to obey the commandments. "If you love me, you will keep my commandments" (John 14:15). He affirmed that He had not come to change the laws of old, "not an iota, not a dot" (Matthew 5:18). In harmony with Adventism, I do not keep the commandments to gain any merit or favor. I find it a privilege to keep His commandments because I love Him and know that He has designed His law of love for my good.

Jesus' reply to the lawyer who asked which were the great commandments shows what we need to obey: "You shall love the Lord your God with all your heart and with all your soul and with all your mind. This is the great and first commandment. And a second is like it: You shall love your neighbor as yourself. On these two commandments depend all the Law and the Prophets" (Matthew 22:37–40).

While loving and obeying God are basic, the commandments that Jesus emphasized, especially in the Sermon on the Mount, were those of the second tablet of the law—those that relate to my conduct towards other people. Jesus spoke specifically of dealing with anger, lust, divorce, oaths, and retaliation (Matthew 5:21–42). At the climax of His sermon, He placed the need for giving to the needy and loving one's enemies (Matthew 5:43–6:4). When I see my church following these instructions in serving the unfortunate at home and abroad, healing the sick in clinics and research hospitals, and educating young people at all levels, I am glad to be an Adventist.

God's people are described in Revelation 14:12 as keeping the "commandments of God" and having "faith in Jesus." The two elements come together: law and Jesus. The first is part of a lifestyle of obedience. The second is the Source of my salvation.

The abundant life

Jesus explained the purpose for His coming: "I came that they may have life and have it abundantly" (John 10:10). This abundant life begins with the peace He gives (John 14:27), a peace that is not simply absence of hostility, but the rest of being yoked together with Jesus. His invitation is clear: "Take my yoke upon you, and learn from me, for I am gentle and lowly in heart, and you will find rest for your souls" (Matthew 11:29).

For me, the biblical doctrine of death sleep, as taught by Jesus and the Seventh-day Adventist Church, adds to my peace. In the story of the resurrection of Lazarus, Jesus told His disciples that Lazarus had "fallen asleep" (John 11:12). Because the disciples misunderstood His figure of speech, Jesus had to tell them clearly, "Lazarus has died" (John 11:14). Being able to commit my loved ones to the sleep of death is possible because Jesus made it clear.

However, the abundant life includes living healthfully, remembering that my body is the temple of the Holy Spirit. It is not my own; I was bought with a price (1 Corinthians 6:19, 20). To me that means that I will follow biblical instructions about eating (Leviticus 7:23, 26; 11). In fact, I am attracted to the Edenic diet: seeds and fruits (Genesis 1:29). Therefore, I am thrilled to belong to a church that follows health principles to the extent that the world recognizes the benefits of the Adventist lifestyle and follows them in careful research.[4]

Following Jesus

Being an Adventist equates with following Jesus. To begin my Christian life, as a member of the Seventh-day Adventist Church, I was baptized by immersion, as He was, thus fulfilling "all righteousness" (Matthew 3:15, 16). As Paul wrote in Romans 6:4, "We were buried therefore with him by baptism into death, in order that, just as Christ was raised from the dead by the glory of the Father, we too might walk in newness of life."

As the disciples gathered in the upper room for the Passover celebration, Jesus washed their dusty feet. He did this to symbolize humility and cleansing, and asked His followers to do likewise: "For I have given you an example, that you also should do just as I have done to you" (John 13:15). I love to emulate Jesus as I participate in the foot-washing ceremony!

As a follower of Jesus, I am a witness to His life, His power, His love.

I can tell others who He is and what He has done for me (Acts 1:8). I join the disciples in receiving and carrying out the gospel commission: "All authority in heaven and on earth has been given to me. Go therefore and make disciples of all nations, baptizing them in the name of the Father and of the Son and of the Holy Spirit, teaching them to observe all that I have commanded you. And behold, I am with you always, to the end of the age" (Matthew 28:18–20). I am grateful to be part of a church that attempts to fulfill this commission worldwide, through proclamation, service, and fellowship.

Prophecy

Jesus believed in prophecy; so do Adventists. The Scriptures, He said, testified of Him (John 5:39). More specifically, He pointed to the writings of Moses as speaking of Him (John 5:46). When the multitude came with the soldiers to arrest Him, Jesus pointed out that "all this has taken place that the Scriptures of the prophets might be fulfilled" (Matthew 26:56). Jesus Himself prophesied. Matthew 24 and 25 record His prophetic utterances about the destruction of Jerusalem and the time of the end.

Jesus promised the coming of "the Helper, the Holy Spirit, whom the Father will send in my name." The purpose of this heavenly Helper, He told His disciples, would be to "teach you all things and bring to your remembrance all that I have said to you" (John 14:26). Prophecy was one of the gifts the Spirit brought to the young church (Romans 12; 1 Corinthians 12). In the book of Revelation, the children of the woman, symbolizing a church, "keep the commandments of God and hold to the testimony of Jesus" (Revelation 12:17). A few chapters later, this "testimony of Jesus" is defined as the "spirit of prophecy" (Revelation

19:10). Prophecy is obviously a mark of those who follow Christ in the end time.

Thus, the importance accorded to the study of the prophetic books of Daniel and Revelation within the Seventh-day Adventist Church, as well as the ministry of Ellen White, harmonizes with Jesus' stance on prophecy.

Jesus in the book of Revelation

From chapter 1 through chapter 22, Jesus is at the center of the book of Revelation. His presence there gives me confidence for the future. He will be Victor. And I may be victorious with Him. My church emphasizes this final victory in Christ.

The book is announced as the "revelation of Jesus Christ" (Revelation 1:1). John watched in awe as Jesus presented Himself in dazzling brightness, walking among the candlesticks, caring for the churches (Revelation 1:12–17). The messages of commendation and warning to the churches of Asia Minor, and through them to the churches of all times, are messages of love and hope.

Jesus then appears as the Lamb that was slain, in the throne scene in chapter 5. Because He has been slain and has ransomed His people by His own blood, He is worthy to open the book. In Revelation 12, Jesus battles the dragon. And He wins!

Yes, there are beasts in Revelation—frightening and powerful beasts. Yet, because of Jesus, there is no fear among His followers. In chapter 14, the Lamb stands victorious with His people on Mount Zion. In chapter 15, the redeemed sing the song of Moses and the Lamb. All nations come to worship Jesus because His "righteous acts have been revealed" (verse

4). A succession of dramatic scenes finally makes way for the appearance of a Rider on a white horse (Revelation 19:11). His robe has been dipped in blood but His name is "King of kings and Lord of lords" (Revelation 19:16). Satan is defeated. Evil comes to an end. The final judgment takes place before the great white throne. John sees a new heaven and a new earth (Revelation 21). Everything is made new. John listens entranced as Jesus reiterates the announcement: "Behold, I am coming soon" (Revelation 22:12).

Together with John, the faithful of all ages, and my fellow Adventists, I look forward to the consummation of all things. On that day, I shall be glad to have walked with Jesus and those who share my love for the Lord. Because of Jesus in the book of Revelation, I have total confidence.

For further reading:
Dederen, Raoul, ed. *Handbook of Seventh-day Adventist Theology*. Commentary Reference Series, vol. 12. Hagerstown, Md.: Review and Herald®, 2000.

General Conference of Seventh-day Adventists, Ministerial Association. *Seventh-day Adventists Believe: A Biblical Exposition of Fundamental Doctrines*. 2nd ed. Nampa, Idaho: Pacific Press®, 2005.

Questions on Doctrine. Annotated Edition. Berrien Springs, Mich.: Andrews University Press, 2003.

Nancy J. Vyhmeister *is retired in Yucaipa, California, after some fifty years of teaching pastors—long term in Chile, Argentina, Philippines, and United States, and for short classes and workshops in another dozen countries. Her areas of expertise have been biblical studies, mission, and research methods. Her doctorate in religious education was granted by Andrews University in 1978. Her publications include articles and books in Spanish and English. Perhaps the best known are* Gramática griega *(editions from 1968 through 2010),* Quality Research Papers *(Zondervan, 2001 and 2008), and* Manual de investigación teológica *(editions from 1980 through Vida, 2009). She edited* Women in Ministry *(Andrews University, 1998). A wife, mother, and grandmother, she is active in local church life.*

References

[1] All Scriptures are quoted from the English Standard Version.

[2] "There is one God: Father, Son, and Holy Spirit, a unity of three co-eternal Persons." Fundamental Belief 2, accessed April 6, 2010, http://www.adventist.org/beliefs/fundamental/index.html.

[3] Ellen G. White, "The Father, Son, and Holy Ghost," *Bible Training School,* March 1, 1906.

[4] Dan Buettner, "The Secrets of Long Life," *National Geographic,* November 2005, 22–26; *The Adventists,* directed by Martin Doblmeier (Alexandria, Va.: Journey Films, 2010), DVD.

MERLIN D. BURT

Chapter 20

Who Was Ellen White?

So who was Ellen White? She was a Christian young adult who with her husband, James White, and Joseph Bates helped found the Seventh-day Adventist Church. She is also a person who received special communications from God in the form of visions and dreams for more than seventy years until her death in 1915. She became an effective writer, whose dozens of spiritually oriented books are still blessing millions of people around the world in more than one hundred languages. Her ministry was influential in the experience of individuals and the ministries of the church. She helped many people to refocus on Jesus and avoid or recover from sinful and destructive life patterns and practices. Her visions and prophetic counsel led in the establishment and growth of Seventh-day Adventist publishing, health, educational ministries, and church organizational structures. But, without a doubt, the most important thing to know about Ellen White was that she was passionately in love with Jesus and was immersed in the Bible. It is this orientation in her writings and experience that has helped so many people to know God and find Jesus as their Savior.

It is also important to know who Ellen White was not. She and other Adventist leaders did not believe that that her prophetic gift gave her authority above or equal with Scripture. She always saw her writings as leading to the Bible. The Bible was the basis for her own faith and her prophetic gift. She consistently and energetically pointed people to the Bible as the only basis for Christian faith and practice. Neither are Ellen White's writings required to establish any of the doctrines of the church. The history of the development of the Seventh-day Adventist Church shows that though her visions enriched understanding and corrected ideas as beliefs developed, they did not originate them. Ellen White was not perfect or free from temptations and struggles. Stress sometimes overwhelmed her and even caused her to become ill. She had marital challenges and struggles with her children, particularly her second son, Edson. Sometimes people view some of Ellen White's writings as hard and critical. It is important to understand that Ellen White did not live in a postmodern world where language almost always remains tentative. Caring Christian people in her day spoke frankly and directly. One more point, though she was a key leader for Seventh-day Adventists, her authority was spiritual rather than official. She did not hold formal offices in the church. Her prophetic and personal experience and ministry gave authority to her writings and counsel.

The remainder of this chapter will focus on the two key motivating forces in Ellen White's life and best answer the question of who she was.

Ellen White and the love of God

Born in 1827, Ellen White grew up in an intensely religious Methodist home. Her father was a class leader and even helped start a branch congregation on the south side of Portland, Maine, during the early 1840s. Ellen's childhood and teenage personality were introverted and intense. She had an active inner life with high personal expectations. She also had some emotionally wrenching religious misconceptions inherited from her religious background. Her belief in an eternally burning hell caused her to view God as a wrathful "tyrant who delighted in the agonies of the condemned."[1] Her reading of pietistic stories of people living saintly lives free from doubts, sins, or emotional weaknesses caused her to doubt whether she could be a Christian. In later life, she described her feeling: "There was in my heart a feeling that I could never become worthy to be called a child of God. . . . A terrible sadness rested on my heart."[2]

Ellen White's youthful conversion spanned a period of years. At the age of nine, a serious injury fractured her nose and perhaps other facial bones. Concentration affected her equilibrium and, in addition, she developed respiratory complications. Her protracted physical disability ended any hope of gaining an education. The grieving process naturally led to anger and resentment, which she projected towards God. "I was un-reconciled to my lot," she recollected, "and at times murmured against the providence of God in thus afflicting me."[3]

Two pivotal experiences in her conversion were realizing that Jesus could save sinners, which she experienced at an 1841 Methodist camp meeting in Buxton, Maine; and finding that God was a loving Father through her interview with Levi Stockman, probably in 1843. At about the same time, she also rejected the idea of an eternally burning hell. "My views of the Father were changed," she remembered, "I now looked upon Him as a kind and tender parent, rather than a stern tyrant compelling men to a blind obedience. My heart went out towards Him in a deep and fervent love."[4] In later years, the love of God became Ellen White's favorite theme.[5] She also taught that it was Jesus' favorite theme.[6] Her favorite song was "Jesus, Lover of My Soul" by John Wesley.[7]

Ellen White's most important and extensive work was her five-volume Conflict of the Ages series. These show from the Bible and history the struggle between good and evil from its beginning until the future new earth when all traces of sin are removed. She named this cosmic struggle the great controversy and framed these five books in terms of God's love. The first book, *Patriarchs and Prophets,* begins with the words: " 'God is Love,' 1 John 4:16. His nature, His law, is love. It ever has been; it ever will be." The last book, *The Great Controversy,* ends with the following words: "One pulse of harmony and gladness beats through the vast creation. . . . From the minutest atom to the greatest world, all things, animate and inanimate, in their unshadowed beauty and perfect joy, declare that God is love."[8] Her most translated and widely read book is *Steps to Christ*. The first chapter of this book is on the love of God.

Ellen White and the Bible

Because of her prophetic visions, Seventh-day Adventists have historically referred to Ellen White's writings as the Spirit of Prophecy. This has sometimes been challenged, but it is essentially accurate if understood correctly and not exclusively limited to Ellen White's ministry and writings. Revelation 19:10 refers to prophetic revelation as the "testimony of Jesus" or the "spirit of prophecy." There is something profound in the words *testimony of Jesus*. In Revelation, John is given the testimony of Jesus to the churches. The words literally convey the meaning that Jesus Himself is communicating with His people through the prophetic messenger. Ellen White understood her own prophetic revelations to be of this character. It was Jesus who was seeking to share testimonies or counsel with His people. The entire prophetic process was and is intrinsically Christ centered.

As one begins to read Ellen White's writings, it is clear they point to the Bible. Ellen White wrote extensively on the relationship of her writings to the Bible and on the role of the Bible in faith and practice. "The Bible," she wrote, "and the Bible alone, is our rule of faith."[9] The conclusion of her first tract—published in 1851—set the tone for her position on the Bible and her writings: "I recommend to you, dear reader, the Word of God as the rule of your faith and practice. By that Word we are to be judged. God has, in that Word, promised to give visions in the 'last days'; not for a new rule of faith, but for the comfort of His people, and to correct those who err from Bible truth."[10]

In 1845, during the first months of her prophetic experience, a prominent minister influenced her to think that her visions were mesmerism—or hypnotism. Once as God's Spirit came upon her, she resisted it. As a result, she was struck dumb, and shown a golden card with fifty texts from the Bible. These texts were burned into her mind and she carefully studied them. God used the Bible to validate her own experience.[11] On at least four occasions during the early years of her prophetic ministry, Ellen White held Bibles in vision.[12] At her last message to the assembled General Conference session in 1909, she held up her Bible before them saying, "Brethren and Sisters, I commend unto you this Book."[13]

Ellen White' writings are closely linked to the Bible. The above-mentioned Conflict of the Ages series is largely a chronological commentary on the Bible. Other books, such as *Christ's Object Lessons* and *Thoughts From the Mount of Blessing,* are commentaries on Jesus' parables and sermons from the Gospels. Her other major books, *Education, The Ministry of Healing,* and *Steps to Christ,* while topically written are firmly rooted in Scripture. Even her counsel books such as the nine-volume *Testimonies for the Church* are strongly Bible oriented.[14] Though she received authoritative prophetic revelations to guide the church and individuals, her first objective was to lead people to the Bible. "Little heed is given to the Bible," she wrote, "and the Lord has given a lesser light to lead men and women to the greater light."[15] When sharing counsel given her by God, she wrote, "It is my first duty to present Bible principles. Then, unless there is a decided, conscientious reform made by those whose cases have been presented before me, I must appeal to them personally."[16]

Ellen White believed in the final authority of Scripture even while she believed that God had spoken to her for the church in a supernatural and prophetic way. The quality of inspiration in her writings is the same as that of Bible prophets, but the purpose is different. A vital part of her special role as a modern prophet was to testify to the centrality and primacy of the Bible. She was a prophet to point Seventh-day Adventists and the world to Scripture. "I have a work of great responsibility to do," she wrote, "to impart by pen and voice the instruction given me, not alone to Seventh-day Adventists, but to the world. . . . This is my work—to open the Scriptures to others as God has opened them to me."[17] The real proof though is in actually reading her writings and connecting with Scripture in a living, dynamic process of faith and action.

Conclusion

I would like to close by refocusing on Ellen White and her relationship with Jesus. In an interview during the last year of her life, she said to her secretary: "I find tears running down my cheeks when I think of what the Lord is to His children, and when I contemplate His goodness, His mercy, [and] His tender compassion."[18]

Adventists today, and particularly young adults, need to see Ellen White as a person who was passionately in love with Jesus. Perhaps the best conclusion would be one further illustration. It is a recollection from Ellen White's oldest granddaughter, Ella Robinson, who was in her early thirties when Ellen White died. When asked her favorite recollection, she said,

> I see grandma standing in the pulpit, dressed in her loose fitting, black sack suit, narrow cuffs of white, narrow white collar secured at the throat by a small brooch. She's been telling of the matchless love of Christ in suffering ignominy and death and even running the risk of eternal separation from His Father in heaven by taking upon Himself the sins of the world. She pauses, looks up, and with one hand resting on the desk and the other lifted heavenward she exclaims in a ringing voice, "Oh, Jesus, how I love you, how I love you, how I love you." There is a deep hush. Heaven is very near.[19]

So who was Ellen White? A woman passionately in love with Jesus and focused on the Bible, who also was called by God to be His prophetic messenger to lead Seventh-day Adventists and the world to the Bible.

She was a spiritual leader who helped establish major ministries of the Seventh-day Adventist Church and her writings continue to give inspired counsel. Wouldn't it be worthwhile to pick up one of her major books and start reading?

For further reading:

Burt, Merlin D. "My Burden Left Me." *Adventist Review*, April 25, 2001, 8–12.

———. "Ellen G. White and Sola Scriptura." http://www .adventistbiblicalresearch.org/conversations%20with%20 presbyterians/Burt,%20Ellen%20White%20&%20Sola%20Scriptura .pdf.

Douglass, Herbert E. *Messenger of the Lord: The Prophetic Ministry of Ellen G. White*. Nampa, Idaho: Pacific Press®, 1998.

Knight, George R. *Reading Ellen White: How to Understand and Apply Her Writings*. Hagerstown, Md.: Review and Herald®, 1997.

Meet Ellen White: A Fascinating Look at Her Personal Life, Prophetic Gift, and Lasting Legacy. DVD. Hagerstown, Md.: Review and Herald®. (Selected from *Keepers of the Flame*). Sydney, Australia: Adventist Media Centre Production, 1996.

White, Arthur L. *Ellen G. White*. 6 vols. Washington, D.C.: Review and Herald®, 1981–1986.

Merlin D. Burt *is the founding director of the integrated Center for Adventist Research at Andrews University. He is also director of the White Estate Branch Office and teaches in the area of Adventist and Ellen White studies. Previous to his present position, he served for ten years as director of the Loma Linda University White Estate Branch Office. He received his PhD from the Andrews University Theological Seminary in 2003. His dissertation covered the development and* *integration of the Sabbath, sanctuary, and Ellen White's role in Sabbatarian Adventism between 1844 and 1849. Previous to his academic and administrative appointments, he served as a pastor in Ohio and California. He and Sarah, his wife of over 30 years, have three children and one grandchild. His hobbies include collecting Adventist related materials and woodworking.*

References

[1] Ellen G. White, "Life Sketches Original Manuscript" (Silver Spring, Md.: Ellen G. White Estate), 32.

[2] Ibid., 14, 15.

[3] James White and Ellen White, *Life Sketches: Ancestry, Early Life, Christian Experience, and Extensive Labors, of Elder James White, and His Wife Mrs. Ellen G. White* (Battle Creek, Mich.: Steam Press of the Seventh-day Adventist Publishing Association, 1880), 135.

[4] Ellen G. White, "Life Sketches Original Manuscript," 43.

[5] Ellen G. White, "The New Zealand Camp Meeting," *Review and Herald,* June 6, 1893, 2, 3.

[6] Ellen G. White, *Christ's Object Lessons* (Washington, D.C.: Review and Herald®, 1941), 40. See also Ellen G. White, *Testimonies for the Church* (Mountain View, Calif.: Pacific Press®, 1948), 6:55.

[7] Ellen G. White to Sister Sisley, October 23, 1906, Letter 324, 1906; "The Work in Oakland and San Francisco, No. 3," *Review and Herald,* December 13, 1906, 10; "The New Zealand Camp Meeting," *Review and Herald,* June 6, 1893.

[8] Ellen G. White, *Patriarchs and Prophets* (Mountain View, Calif.: Pacific Press®, 1958), 33; *The Great Controversy* (Mountain View, Calif.: Pacific Press®, 1939), 678.

[9] Ellen G. White, *Counsels on Sabbath School Work* (Washington, D.C.: Review and Herald®, 1938), 84.

[10] Ellen G. White, *A Sketch of the Christian Experience and Views of Ellen G. White* (Saratoga Springs, N.Y.: James White, 1851), 64.

[11] Ellen G. White, *Early Writings* (Hagerstown, Md.: Review and Herald®, 2000), 22, 23.

[12] W. C. White to Sarah Peck, April 2, 1919, Center for Adventist Research, Andrews University, Berrien Springs, Michigan (CAR); J. N. Loughborough, *The Great Second Advent Movement: Its Rise and Progress* (Washington, D.C.: Review and Herald®, 1905), 236, 237; Otis Nichol, "Statement by Otis Nichol," n.d., CAR; Ellen G. White, "My Christian Experience: Views and Labors in Connection With the Rise and Progress of the Third Angel's Message," *Spiritual Gifts,* vol. 2 (Battle Creek, Mich.: James White, 1860), 75–79; James White to Leonard and Elvira Hastings, August 26, 1848; Mrs. S. Howland, Rebecca Howland Winslow, Frances Howland Lunt, "Signed Statement," Manuscript release no. 1148.

[13] Quoted in W. A. Spicer, *The Spirit of Prophecy in the Advent Movement* (Washington, D.C.: Review and Herald®, 1937), 30.

[14] Ellen White, *Testimonies for the Church,* 9 vols. (Mountain View, Calif.: Pacific Press®, 1948).

[15] Ellen White, "An Open Letter From Mrs. E. G. White to All Who Love the Blessed Hope," *Review and Herald,* January 20, 1903, 15.

[16] Ellen White, Letter 69, 1896, quoted in *Selected Messages,* bk. 3 (Washington D.C.: Review and Herald®, 1980), 30.

[17] Ellen White, *Testimonies for the Church,* 8:236.

[18] Ellen White interview with C. C. Crisler, July 21, 1914.

[19] Oral interview between James R. Nix and Ella Mae Robinson, October 12, 1979.

IF YOU ENJOYED ALWAYS PREPARED, YOU'LL WANT TO READ . . .

Understanding Creation

For centuries Western culture operated within the context of a Christian worldview. For this reason, the answer to any question was anchored in the belief that God exists and is the Creator and Sustainer of all, and that the Bible is a trustworthy revelation of God. Many of the founders of modern science, including Copernicus, Galileo, Kepler, Pascal, Boyle, Newton, and Halley, were believers of those central concepts. During the past 200 years, our culture, particularly the scientific community, has been moving away from the Christian worldview, and assuming a naturalistic stance that discounts any supernatural intervention in the origin, functioning, and maintenance of our world. As a result, two opposing philosophical views contend for allegiance today. *Understanding Creation* articulates twenty questions about faith and science that Christians often encounter. The coeditors have assembled an international group of experienced scientists, researchers, and thinkers who provide thoughtful answers to these questions. They all share several convictions: the biblical record is an essential component of Christian doctrine; Christian faith and empirical science can work fruitfully together; and our comprehension of truth is progressive.

Edited by HUMBERTO RASI *and* JAMES GIBSON

Answers to questions on faith and science.

Hardcover, 224 Pages
ISBN 13: 978-0-8163-2428-6
ISBN 10: 0-8163-2428-X

Pacific Press® Publishing Association
"Where the Word Is Life"

Three ways to order:
1. Local | Adventist Book Center®
2. Call | 1-800-765-6955
3. Shop | AdventistBookCenter.com